# Dambuster
# Crash Sites

# Dambuster Crash Sites

617 Dambuster Squadron Crash Sites
in Holland and Germany

Chris Ward and Andreas Wachtel

Pen & Sword
**AVIATION**

First published in Great Britain in 2007 by
Pen & Sword Aviation
an imprint of
Pen & Sword Books Ltd

Copyright © Chris Ward, 2007

ISBN 978 1 84415 568 2

A CIP catalogue record for this book is
available from the British Library

Typeset in Palatino by
Phoenix Typesetting, Auldgirth, Dumfriesshire

Printed and bound in England by
CPI UK

Pen & Sword Books Ltd incorporates the Imprints of Pen & Sword Aviation,
Pen & Sword Maritime, Pen & Sword Military, Wharncliffe Local History,
Pen & Sword Select, Pen & Sword Military Classics and Leo Cooper.

For a complete list of Pen & Sword titles please contact
PEN & SWORD BOOKS LIMITED
47 Church Street, Barnsley, South Yorkshire, S70 2AS, England
E-mail: enquiries@pen-and-sword.co.uk
Website: www.pen-and-sword.co.uk

# Contents

# Introduction

There can be little doubt that the bombing operation carried out against four of Germany's dams in May 1943 became the most celebrated feat of arms in aviation history. At the time it captured the imagination of the free world, and provided a boost to the morale of the war-weary British, in whose favour the tide had only recently begun to turn after years of bad news. Since the war, Operation *Chastise* has continued to captivate generations of people around the world, and the hunger for knowledge does not abate. Enthusiasts for the subject demand detail. It is not enough for them to know that eight of the specially modified Lancasters failed to return. They want to understand the circumstances behind the losses, and I strove to provide answers to their questions in my book, *Dambusters*, published by Red Kite in 2003. There are those, though, who are not content to simply read about history, but desire also to experience it for themselves as far as it is possible so long after the event. For them it is necessary actually to see the places connected with this story of courage and determination, to soak up the atmosphere and to pay their respects in person. The dams, the crash sites and the cemeteries all possess their own aura, and act as a magnet to draw people on a journey of discovery. I know from personal experience what it is to stand on the Möhne and Eder Dams for the very first time, after reading and rereading the accounts in a multitude of books since childhood. I was seven years old when I first learned of the Dambusters, and almost forty when I caught my first excited glimpse of the Möhne through a coach window. My heart was thumping at the fulfilment of a life-long ambition, but I had to wait another half-hour before I could actually set foot on the dam, as the driver had missed the coach park entrance and had to detour around the lake. I remember the frustration welling up inside me as we wasted those precious minutes crossing the Delecke and Körbacher bridges to bring us back to our starting point. It was all forgotten, of course, as I stood on the centre of the dam, oblivious to all the other tourists and promenaders about me. As I faced the Heversberg, the spit of land a mile away across the smooth waters of the lake from where the bombing runs began, I was totally engrossed in recalling to mind the tense narrative of Paul Brickhill's account of the attacks that took place in the earliest hours of Monday 17 May 1943. I can still recall the power of my emotions on that day, and each time I have visited a new location while researching the squadron's history, that sense of excitement, of capturing a piece of history, has returned. It is a pilgrimage by the faithful to honour fallen heroes, whose names have become so familiar over the years. To borrow the immortal words of Abraham Lincoln, spoken at Gettysburg, Pennsylvania, in November 1863, 'it is altogether fitting and proper that we should do this'.

It is assumed that readers of this book intend to use it as a guide to visit the places documented, and are already broadly familiar with the events of Operation *Chastise* and the attack on the Dortmund-Ems Canal. For this reason I have not included an account of each operation, but rather outlined the involvement of each of the crews who failed to return, and the circumstances of their demise. The Dams cost the squadron eight out of nineteen crews, or 42 per cent of those dispatched, while the Dortmund-Ems Canal cost five out of eight, and if one includes the loss of S/L Maltby on the previous night when the Lancasters were recalled while outbound for the canal, the casualty figure becomes six out of nine, or 66 per cent of those dispatched. A number of founder crews, including survivors of the Dams raid, were present on this operation, and were among those failing to return. The two operations have been combined in this book because they are similar in a number of respects, and took place in roughly the same geographic region of Germany and Holland, making them easily within reach of each other. Both were attacks on aquatic-related targets, both were conducted at very low level, and together they represent the fortunes of 617 Squadron in 1943 before the Cheshire era. Those killed are mostly buried in the Commonwealth War Graves Commission cemeteries at Reichswald and Rheinberg in Germany, and Bergen-op-Zoom in Holland, while others lie in local cemeteries in Holland.

As always, I am indebted to my friend Andreas Wachtel. Without his unselfish hard work and commitment to keeping alive the memory of the courageous young men depicted in this book, and *Dambusters*, both publications would have been much the poorer.

Finally, may I add for the benefit of those who wonder about their reception by our former enemies in Germany, that in my frequent visits to the country to carry out research, I have encountered only friendliness, courtesy and a willingness to help. The German people seem less aware of the Second World War, or are, at least, less willing to hold on to the memory of it, but in no way, in my experience at least, harbour any resentment towards the British. It was an intensely painful period in Germany's history, and they are content to let it go. It is for the victors to remember, but to do so in a respectful way, particularly as guests in their country.

Chris Ward
Lutterworth.
December 2006

# Roll of Honour

**Key**
(C) – RCAF
(A) – RAAF
(NZ) – RNZAF
* – Bar
MID – Mentioned in Dispatches

## Operation *Chastise* 16/17 May 1943

### Lancaster ED934 AJ-K

| | |
|---|---|
| Pilot | P/O V.W. Byers (C) |
| Flight engineer | Sgt A.J. Taylor |
| Navigator | P/O J.H. Warner |
| Wireless operator | Sgt J. Wilkinson |
| Bomb-aimer | Sgt A.N. Whitaker |
| Front gunner | Sgt J. McA. Jarvie |
| Rear gunner | Sgt J. McDowell (C) |

### Lancaster ED864 AJ-B

| | |
|---|---|
| Pilot | F/L W. Astell DFC |
| Flight engineer | Sgt J. Kinnear |
| Navigator | P/O F.A. Wile (C) |
| Wireless operator | Sgt A. Garshowitz (C) |
| Bomb-aimer | F/O D. Hopkinson |
| Front gunner | Sgt F.A. Garbas (C) |
| Rear gunner | Sgt R. Bolitho |

### Lancaster ED927 AJ-E

| | |
|---|---|
| Pilot | F/L R.N.G. Barlow DFC(A) |
| Flight engineer | Sgt S.L.Whillis |
| Navigator | F/O P.S. Burgess |
| Wireless operator | F/O C.R. Williams DFC (A) |
| Bomb-aimer | Sgt A. Gillespie DFM |
| Front gunner | F/O H.S. Glinz (C) |
| Rear gunner | Sgt J.R.G. Liddell |

### Lancaster ED925 AJ-M

| | |
|---|---|
| Pilot | F/L J.V. Hopgood DFC* |
| Flight engineer | Sgt C. Brennan |
| Navigator | F/O K. Earnshaw (C) |
| Wireless operator | Sgt J.W. Minchin |
| Front gunner | P/O G.H.F.G. Gregory DFM |

### Lancaster ED865 AJ-S

| | |
|---|---|
| Pilot | P/O L.J. Burpee DFM (C) |
| Flight engineer | Sgt G. Pegler |
| Navigator | Sgt T. Jaye |
| Wireless operator | P/O L.G. Weller |
| Bomb-aimer | Sgt J.L. Arthur (C) |
| Front gunner | Sgt W.C.A. Long |
| Rear gunner | F/S J.G. Brady (C) |

### Lancaster ED910 AJ-C

| | |
|---|---|
| Pilot | P/O W. Ottley DFC |
| Flight engineer | Sgt R. Marsden |
| Navigator | F/O J.K. Barrett DFC |
| Wireless operator | Sgt J. Guterman DFM |
| Bomb-aimer | F/S T.B. Johnston |
| Front gunner | Sgt H.J. Strange |

### Lancaster ED937 AJ-Z

| | |
|---|---|
| Pilot | S/L H.E. Maudslay DFC |
| Flight engineer | Sgt J. Marriott DFM |
| Navigator | F/O R.A. Urquhart DFC (C) |
| Wireless operator | Sgt L.W. Nichols |
| Bomb-aimer | P/O M.J.D. Fuller |
| Front gunner | F/O W.J. Tytherleigh DFC |
| Rear gunner | Sgt J.R. Burrows |

### Lancaster ED887 AJ-A

| | |
|---|---|
| Pilot | S/L H.M. Young DFC* |
| Flight engineer | Sgt D.T. Horsfall |
| Navigator | Sgt C.W. Roberts |
| Wireless operator | Sgt A.P. Cottam (C) |
| Bomb-aimer | F/O V.S. MacCausland (C) |
| Front gunner | Sgt G.A. Yeo |
| Rear gunner | Sgt W. Ibbotson |

## Dortmund-Ems Canal 14/15 September 1943 (Aborted)

### Lancaster JA981 KC-J

| | |
|---|---|
| Pilot | S/L D.J.H. Maltby DSO DFC |
| Flight engineer | Sgt W. Hatton |
| Navigator | F/S V. Nicholson DFM |
| Wireless operator | F/S A.J. Stone |
| Bomb-aimer | P/O J. Fort DFC |
| Gunner | Sgt V. Hill |

| Gunner | W/O J.L. Welch DFM |
|--------|--------------------|
| Gunner | H.T. Simmonds |

## Dortmund-Ems Canal 15/16 September 1943

### Lancaster EE144 AJ-S

| Pilot | W/C G.W. Holden DSO DFC* MID |
|-------|------------------------------|
| Flight engineer | Sgt D.J.D. Powell MID |
| Navigator | F/L T.H. Taerum DFC (C) |
| Wireless operator | F/L R.E.G. Hutchison DFC* |
| Bomb-aimer | F/O F.M. Spafford DFC DFM (A) |
| Gunner | P/O G.A. Deering DFC (C) |
| Gunner | F/O H.J. Pringle DFC |
| Gunner | P/O T.A. Meikle DFM |

### Lancaster EE130 AJ-A

| Pilot | F/L R.A.P. Allsebrook DSO DFC |
|-------|-------------------------------|
| Flight engineer | F/S P. Moore |
| Navigator | P/O N.A. Botting |
| Wireless operator | F/O J.M. Grant DFC |
| Bomb-aimer | F/S R.B.S. Lulham |
| Gunner | Sgt I.G. Jones |
| Gunner | F/S W. Walker |
| Gunner | F/S S. Hitchen |

### Lancaster JA874 KC-E

| Pilot | P/O W.G. Divall |
|-------|------------------|
| Flight engineer | Sgt E.C.A. Blake |
| Navigator | F/O D.W. Warwick (C) |
| Wireless operator | F/S J.S. Simpson |
| Bomb-aimer | F/S R.C. McArthur |
| Gunner | Sgt A.A. Williams |
| Gunner | Sgt G.S. Miles |
| Gunner | Sgt D. Allatson |

### Lancaster JA898 KC-X

| Pilot | F/L H.S. Wilson |
|-------|------------------|
| Flight engineer | P/O T.W. Johnson |
| Navigator | F/O J.A. Rodger |
| Wireless operator | W/O L. Mieyette (C) |
| Bomb-aimer | F/O G.H. Coles (C) |
| Gunner | F/S T.H. Payne |
| Gunner | Sgt G.M. Knox |
| Gunner | F/S E. Hornby |

### Lancaster JB144 KC-N

| Pilot | F/L L.G. Knight DSO MID (A) |
|-------|------------------------------|

# CHAPTER 1

# The Tourist's Guide

Andreas Wachtel and I have derived great pleasure and satis-faction from our research of and visits to the events and locations mentioned in this book. Now it is your turn to follow in our humble footsteps and enjoy the beauty and hospitality of these regions of Germany and Holland. Andreas has pains-takingly compiled directions to the crash sites, while Clare Bennett and Julian Maslin have done likewise for the cemeteries. As most of the sites are within the same general region of Germany and Holland, I have chosen to present them in alphabetical order, rather than deal with them by operation. The difficulty for Andreas was finding a starting point for each route, as visitors will select their own places to stay. He has chosen motorways, which anyone can follow on a road map, and should one approach a specific junction mentioned in the guide from the opposite direction to that described by Andreas, it can be simply adjusted. Now let me tell you the story of one of the crash sites by way of an explanation of how Andreas and I began our quest to find and document them all.

At a rural spot in Germany, a little to the north-west of Hamm in the district of Heesen, and at the point where a field and wood meet, there stood a tall but simple wooden cross and a memorial stone set in flowers in a small crater. The stone bears an inscription:

BEWAHRT DEN FRIEDEN – KRIEG IST GRAUSAM.
Preserve peace, war is cruel.

For most of the autumn and winter months the crater was water-logged and the original cross became rotten. Now, however, a new cross has been erected above the crater, and this was dedicated in May 2007 in the presence of the authors and members of their tour party, along with an RAF contingent from Brize Norton and German representatives. It is a peaceful and picturesque location not visible from the road, and has been the site of the memorial now for more than twenty-five years. It marks the spot where P/O Ottley and five of his crew died at 02.35 on Monday 17 May 1943 on their way to the Sorpe Dam. There are thousands of crash sites in Germany, a very few marked in some way, while the vast majority are now totally erased. The fact that this one exists at all and is lovingly maintained throughout the year is due to the devotion of a few German people, who decided that the passing of these young men and former enemies on this lonely piece of ground should not go unmarked. In an article written for the *Heesen Gazette* the late Bernard Droste explained the history of this memorial.

> In December 1980 the Dambuster Research Centre in Great Britain was given the task of ascertaining the exact crash site of Lancaster bomber AJ-C. I was then able through enquiries to trace the crash site on the northern edge of Ostbusch. That is how it came to be, that a memorial to peace was erected here. The project was undertaken by local scouts, British soldiers stationed at Hamm, and representatives of the Heesen Catholic Church, the town of Hamm, British Transport workshop and 617 Squadron. The crater caused by the bomb explosion had over the years been filled in with building rubble, scrap cars and washing machines, which, once removed, enabled the site to be again recognisable as a crater. Heinrich Hemmis made a remembrance cross from the trunk of one of the oak trees growing in the Ostbusch, and Heinrich Möllenbrink donated the boulder carrying the inscription. The cross was dedicated on the 26th of September 1981 in a ceremony conducted by the Rural Dean in the presence of a member

of the protestant clergy, the Mayor of Wieland, scouts, soldiers and many other people who came from near and far. The rear gunner of the Lancaster that crashed here also came, Fred Tees, who, by a miracle, survived the crash. He came from England with a Dutch friend following an invitation from Heesen. It was impressive, that here at the site of such horror, former enemies stood next to one another now as friends, and shared in different languages the preserving of peace and the Lord's Prayer. Six months later, in Letchworth, Hertfordshire, Fred Tees died.

Bernard Droste, a retired senior policeman, became responsible for the care of the site, before handing over to others. He died in 1998. From the early nineties the memorial was lovingly tended by a local couple, Günther and Marianne Borstelmann, and a lifelong friendship has developed between them and those from England who have regularly visited the site as part of the Shortland Dams Tour. Barbara Rayner and Derek Windmill, both of them guides at the Lincolnshire Aviation Heritage Centre at East Kirkby, have cultivated a special bond of friendship with the Borstelmanns, and exchange letters and information on a regular basis. Günther was born in Oranienburg near Berlin in 1937, and he and Marianne married in 1974 and lived in Lüneburg. On retiring from his work as a psychiatric nurse in 1989, Günther moved with Marianne to a new home at Heesen, near Marianne's beloved hometown of Hamm. While Germany was divided it was always a difficult process for them to visit Günther's relatives in Oranienburg in the east, but then, after reunification, a twist of fate and coincidence had Hamm and Oranienburg twinned. Marianne has been honoured by the German State for her incredible service to humanity as a blood donor. I have met Günther and Marianne on a number of occasions, both during ceremonies at the memorial at Heesen and when they visited the Lincolnshire Aviation Heritage Centre at East Kirkby, and can testify personally to their genuine warmth and generosity of heart. They spared no effort in their preparations to receive their visitors from England for the annual ceremony on the edge of the wood, and their welcome and open affection left few dry eyes. Along with members of their family and friends they lugged tables and benches to the small clearing, and provided enough food and drink to cater for double the thirty-five or so who attended. Sadly, ill health now prevents these lovely people from continuing their work, but others have become involved and the memorial will be maintained.

My desire to visit the crash sites resulting from the Dams and Dortmund-Ems Canal operations was born out of the need to understand the circumstances of the losses, in order to accurately convey the information to those reading my book, *Dambusters*. Gradually, though, it became something more, and perhaps the catalyst for this was my first visit to Ottley's crash site in 2000. As described previously, I encountered genuine compassion and humanity, which transcended nationalities. It makes no difference to Günther and Marianne that they honour former enemies, as they desire only to mark the passing of six young lives and bring former enemies together. I began to wonder how many people had stood at other places where the lives of similar young men had been extinguished in an instant in the cause of freedom. I knew of course from reading about 617 Squadron, that many of the sites associated with the deaths of its members had never been investigated, and this meant that the precise circumstances of their passing remained hidden. I wanted to bring their final moments to light both for the sake of history and as a gesture of respect for their sacrifice. With a massive amount of help from Andreas and some also from Horst Münter, our aviation archaeologist friend from Dortmund, I have been able to visit all of the accessible locations in Germany and Holland described in this book. What follows is your guide to them.

# CHAPTER 2

# F/L R.A.P. Allsebrook
## EE130, AJ-A
### Bergeshövede/Bevergern, in the 'Nasses Dreieck', Wet Triangle

### Dortmund–Ems Canal Raid

Ralph Allsebrook came to 617 Squadron as something of a veteran, having begun his operational career with 49 Squadron at Scampton back in the Hampden days. On the night of 14/15 February 1942, his crew had been one of ninety-eight dispatched to Mannheim for an area attack on the city, the first such indiscriminate raid to be officially sanctioned since the issuing of the controversial area bombing directive by the Air Ministry earlier that very day. At least part of the return journey was undertaken on one engine, and this failed as the south coast of England hove into sight. A successful ditching was carried out and the crew took to their dinghy, which was spotted by a Beaufighter crew returning from a patrol. They were soon picked up by a coastguard launch, but three of them had by then suffered frostbite in the freezing conditions. As a Flying Officer, Allsebrook was awarded a DFC in April 1942, just as the trusty Hampden was being replaced by the unpopular Manchester. He

A unique photograph of the recovery by the German military of
Ralph Allesbrook's Lancaster from the waters of the Wet
Triangle at Bergeshövede, the meeting point of the Dortmund-
Ems and Mittelland Canals.

returned to 49 Squadron for a second tour at the end of January
1943 as a Flight Lieutenant, and operated against Hamburg on
3/4 February, when he experienced an engine fire over the
target. Two trips to Lorient in mid month sandwiched one to
Milan, and the month ended with operations against Cologne
and St Nazaire. By the end of the first week of March Allsebrook
and his crew had added to their tally with sorties to Berlin,
Hamburg and Essen, and then they operated against
Nuremberg, Munich and Stuttgart during the course of the
following six nights. The pace slackened somewhat for them in
April and May before their posting to 617 Squadron.

It was one minute past midnight on 16 September 1943, when
Allsebrook took off from Coningsby at the head of the second of
two sections of four aircraft bound for the Dortmund-Ems Canal
near Ladbergen. The two sections were to fly independently of
each other on broadly parallel headings until reaching a
*rendezvous* point near the target at Wettringen. It is assumed that
all went well at first, and landfall was made on the Dutch coast

At the midpoint of the left-hand edge of the picture are three figures, one of whom is Frau Erika Kaiser, who lives to this day in the house on the quayside where she was resident at the time of the incident in September 1943. The photographs were donated by her and are reproduced with her kind permission.

with the section comprising Allsebrook, Shannon, Divall and Rice intact and on course. We know from Martin's account, that a blanket of fog descended like a wall as the first wave crossed into Germany, and we can assume the second wave encountered the same conditions. It would have become clear that a *rendezvous* was impossible, and the two sections, even perhaps individual aircraft, navigated their way to the target almost independently. It is clear from the location of the crash sites of both Lancasters from this section that they had not located the briefed aiming point, and were about ten miles too far north. This is entirely understandable in the circumstances, when the ground might appear only fleetingly and intermittently. An additional problem was the network of streams, rivers and canals criss-crossing the region, which had to be identified. Following the loss of W/C Holden *en route*, (see Chapter 8) Allsebrook assumed command of the operation, and he was heard to make a number of radio transmissions authorising F/L Wilson and P/O Divall to carry

The crane on the quayside of the Wet Triangle, which was
knocked into the water by Allesbrook's Lancaster.

out their attacks. Sometime around 02.20 BST Allsebrook crashed
into the triangular basin at Bergeshövede where the Mittelland
and Dortmund-Ems canals meet. Eyewitnesses described the
Lancaster being engaged by flak and losing part of a wing. It was
on fire as it crested the Huckberg and dropped towards the quayside on the north side of Das Nasse Dreieck, the Wet Triangle. It
clipped the roof of the house at the end of the row at the foot of
the hill, collided with a crane, flipped over and fell into the water.
The 12,000-lb bomb was not on board the Lancaster at the time of
the crash, and there was no report of it exploding anywhere
within earshot of the neighbouring villages. There is no question
that had it exploded, it would have shattered windows within a
mile radius. The German authorities produced a highly detailed
drawing of the bomb, which was being employed for the first
time, and, in view of the fact that all the other bombs from this
operation were accounted for, the conclusion is that Allsebrook's
bomb was jettisoned or simply failed to detonate, and was subse-
quently recovered by the German military.

Route Map of the Dortmund-Ems Canal operation; solid lines show routes to the target, and dotted lines return flight paths
The first group, which included Les Knight's plane, flew the "A" route while the second group followed the "B" route

The intended routes to the Dortmund-Ems Canal on the night of the 15/16th September 1943. The southerly track is that adopted by Allsebrook's section.

## Tour Guide

It was on a Monday in May 2002 that Andreas and I headed for Bergeshövede, so I could meet with *Frau* Erika Kaiser and hear her account of Allsebrook's end. When we arrived at this peaceful and picturesque corner of Germany we found representatives of two local newspapers waiting for us at *Frau* Kaiser's house, along with her son Bernhard, serving at that time in a helicopter unit in the German military. Also present were a

The lock gates looking towards the Wet Triangle.

local historian, *Herr* Uphoff, and an extra interpreter for good measure. We all sat round a table for a discussion, and we provided the two lady reporters with a basic account of the attack on the Dortmund-Ems Canal, with details of the crews and casualties. Andreas couldn't resist expounding his well thought-out and balanced view of Bomber Command's offensives to one of them, who clearly held the official German opinion that the bombing was carried out in vengeance to kill women and children. Andreas ran rings round her, and she looked uncomfortable, but I doubt her deeply ingrained ideas will have been changed. For all that, it was a useful and pleasant experience, which enabled me better to describe the events of 1943 in my book *Dambusters*.

Coming from the direction of Osnabrück, we travel towards the Dutch border along the A30 (E30) as far as exit 10 (Hörstel). At the T-junction we turn right onto the K38 in the direction of Riesenbeck and Bergeshövede. Further along its course the K38

The Wet Triangle from its western end. The Mittelland Canal enters the basin centre picture.

The old footbridge over the narrow channel.

The Wet Triangle and quayside.

The quayside. The guesthouse Zum Nassen Dreieck is the
tallest building centre right.

An RAF reconnaissance photo at the memorial at Gravenhorst.

curves sharply to the left before crossing the Mittelland Canal by means of a bridge. Shortly before the bridge on the right is a narrow road. Take this road and soon after the sharp right-hand bend you come across the restaurant/guesthouse, Zum Nassen Dreieck, on the right. One can park in the parking spot in front of the above establishment and walk through to the quayside, or walk/drive round the side onto the quayside, where parking is also available. Standing with one's back to the restaurant facing south, to the left at about a 10 o'clock position the Dortmund-Ems Canal enters the Wet Triangle. To the right the twin channels of the Dortmund-Ems Canal depart the Wet Triangle in a westerly direction. At the left-hand end of the quay the towpath follows the course of the Mittelland Canal northwards. We turn to the right and walk along the canal and an old lock gate. The path leads past an old bunker and begins a slight upward incline. At the top of the rise a path branches off to the left to a wonderfully restored bridge. Walk to the mid point of the bridge, which,

A photo of the Mittelland Canal at Gravenhorst after the
first RAF attack in late 1944.

The memorial at Gravenhorst.

The memorial at Gravenhorst.

incidentally, dates from the time of Wilhelm II, and look towards the Wet Triangle. Allsebrook's Lancaster came over the wooded hill to the left, and was already on fire. He attempted to clear the house at the far right end beyond the guesthouse. He struck the roof of the house (the repair is easily identifiable today by the different tiles), careered into a quayside crane, toppling it into the water, and crashed inverted into the basin in front of the lock gates.

Before departing the area it is worthwhile to make a very short detour to a memorial commemorating the 5 Group attacks on the Mittelland Canal at Gravenhorst, literally only a five-minute drive away. We journey back along the narrow road to the K38, turn right onto it and drive across the bridge spanning the Mittelland Canal. At the T-junction we turn left onto the K17 and head towards Gravenhorst. After passing under the *Autobahn* we arrive at a T-junction with the L594. We turn left along the L594 in the direction of Hörstel. After a few metres, and just before reaching another bridge across the Mittelland Canal, a small tarmac road leads off to the left. We take this and it brings us back under the L594, with the canal running parallel literally a few metres to our left. Shortly after the underpass we come across the memorial, a circle of bombs, on our right. Within the circle are reconnaissance photos showing the devastation caused by the bombing by 5 Group in late 1944 and early 1945.

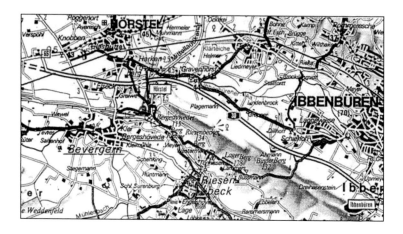

Ralph Allsebrook, 3rd from left, and his crew when serving with 49 Squadron.

# CHAPTER 3

# F/L W. Astell
## ED864, AJ-B
## Near Marbeck, North of Raesfeld

### Dams Raid

Earmarked to be S/L Young's deputy as A Flight commander
at 617 Squadron, William (Bill) Astell was born in 1920 at
Peover in Cheshire to an upper class family. By the 1930s the
family was resident in Chapel-en-le-Frith on the edge of
the Peak District of Derbyshire. His father, Godfrey, was the
managing director of J & N Philips, a textile company, which he
ran from its main site in Church Street, Manchester. His
mother's sister was a member of the Dundas family, whose
sons (and therefore Bill's cousins) John and Hugh flew Spitfires
during the Battle of Britain. John was killed, but Hugh survived
to become the RAF's youngest ever Group Captain, and as Sir
Hugh he became Chairman of the BET Group and Thames tele-
vision during the 1980s.

The Astell family's affluence enabled Bill to travel extensively
overseas to broaden his education and experience, and in 1936,
at the age of sixteen, he sailed to Canada to visit relatives. He
also took a trip to the White Sea in a trawler. He spent the end
of 1937, most of 1938 and the first half of 1939 in Germany and

France, and on his return to England he joined the RAF Air Reserve, undergoing training at an airfield in nearby Staffordshire. In September 1939 he was posted to Hastings to continue his training, before being posted to Salisbury, Southern Rhodesia, at the end of April 1940. He was awarded his wings in January 1941, passing out as a Pilot Officer, and he was immediately posted for duty in Malta. Before he had an opportunity to see action in the war, however, he was struck down by typhoid, and was forced to spend time first in hospital and then convalescing.

He finally joined 148 Squadron at Kabrit in Egypt in May 1941 and began operations as a Wellington pilot, attacking ports and landing grounds. A crash on 30 November left him with burns to his body, mostly his back, and cuts to his scalp and face, and although he did not consider himself to be seriously injured, he remained in hospital until February 1942. This was followed by a month's sick leave, which he spent in Kenya, before returning to duty with 148 Squadron and a new crew in March.

On the last night of May 1942 Astell took off to attack an enemy landing ground and failed to return, triggering the obligatory telegram to his family. Five days later Astell walked in to report being attacked by an enemy fighter over the target. Apart from wounding two of his crew, the engagement left his Wellington with an unserviceable rear turret and rudder controls, and a fire in the fuselage, starboard wing and engine nacelle. He ordered his crew to bale out, and four of them had time to comply before they ran out of altitude. Astell pulled off a crash-landing, and he and his navigator, P/O 'Bishop' Dodds, a former cleric, emerged from the wreckage with minor burns and began walking. After a few days a British patrol was spotted, and Astell moved forward to make contact, leaving his now ailing navigator hidden. He failed to make contact on this occasion, and was unable to relocate his navigator when he went back for him. Two days later Astell was picked up by Arabs and pointed in the direction of the British lines. He spent a few days in hospital in Tobruk, before being sent home via America, arriving back in England aboard the *Queen Mary* in September.

He was posted to Wigsley in Nottinghamshire, one of 5

Group's training stations, and also spent time at Hullavington and Fulbeck. Now with the rank of Flight Lieutenant, he was posted to 57 Squadron at Scampton on 25 January 1943 to undertake a second tour, this time on Lancasters, and it was here that he acquired his new crew. Operations followed to Milan, Nuremberg, Cologne, Berlin, Hamburg and Essen. After grabbing some sleep on return from the last mentioned on the night of 5/6 March, he went home on leave for what turned out to be the last time during his 57 Squadron service.

He returned to his squadron on 12 March and was posted to 617 Squadron on 25 March, not knowing what lay ahead. He managed one more spell of leave during the Dams training period, and while visiting his father at work, he accidentally ran into one of the secretaries, knocking her over and scattering papers over the floor. Picking her up he kissed her on the cheek, telling her he would see her on his next leave, with the prospect of that occurring after the operation for which they were preparing. All who knew Astell, particularly those of the fairer sex, would testify to his open, friendly, charming nature, which made him immensely likeable.

Astell's crew was fairly typical of those posted in as founder members of 617 Squadron, and it is interesting to delve a little more deeply into their individual backgrounds as representative of the squadron as a whole. Five of the crew had been together at 1654 Conversion Unit (CU) at Wigsley from October 1942 until their posting to 9 Squadron at Waddington two days before Christmas. They were navigator Floyd Wile, bomb-aimer Don Hopkinson, wireless operator Al Garshowitz and gunners Frank Garbas and Richard Bolitho. At Waddington they were teamed up with a Sgt Stephenson as their pilot, with whom they flew for the first time on Christmas Eve, carrying out circuits and landings. This association was not destined to last long, however, although Sgt Stephenson's disappearance from the scene is a little confusing. On the night of 8/9 January 1943 a 9 Squadron Lancaster failed to return from a raid on Duisburg, and Sgt Foote and his crew were all killed. Listed as the crew's flight engineer was Sgt M.W. Stephenson, who is assumed to be the pilot mentioned above. In 9 Squadron records, though, he is shown as a flight engineer, and not as a pilot flying as second dickey. There were seven men on board the missing Lancaster, not eight as was normal when a second pilot was being carried. Sgt Foote's regular flight engineer was not on the trip, and this leaves us with the conclusion that, if these Stephensons are one and the same, he must have volunteered to act as flight engineer at short notice. Had he survived, matters might have turned out differently for his former crew.

Floyd Wile was one of three Canadians in the crew. He was born in Nova Scotia in April 1919, the fifth of seven children. Following high school he worked on the land as a farm hand and in the lumber industry. He had shown an interest in radio during his youth and actually studied the subject for a year at technical school. He was also keen on sporting activities, particularly skiing, skating and swimming. Before enlisting in the RCAF he joined a local army unit in Yarmouth, Nova Scotia, but resigned after a month. At 5 Initial Training School he was noted as being slow thinking, hard working, the plodder type, while at No. 8 Air Observer School he was described as average, with the comment, 'in no respect has he shown much aptitude for work'. Another report described him as a quiet lad, and backward through lack of experience in mixing. Three months later, however, his commanding officer at No. 9 Bombing and Gunnery School called him outstanding and a brilliant trainee, who was very popular and had good self control. Despite this he passed out of No. 2 Air Navigation School with a 'not outstanding, average NCO material' tag, but was commissioned as a Pilot Officer before leaving Wigsley in December 1942.

The other Canadians in Astell's crew were Abram Garshowitz (known within his family as Albert or Al) and Frank Garbas, who were great boyhood friends. Al was the ninth of twelve children, and was born in Hamilton, Ontario, in December 1921. He went to school locally, and afterwards worked in the family business selling new and used furniture. Frank Garbas was born in July 1922, ten years after his parents arrived in Canada from their native Poland. He was the fifth of nine children. Once in Canada the letter 'z' was dropped from the family name Garbasz, while his father became Stanley rather than Stanislaus. Even so, family life revolved around Polish traditions, religion and cuisine, and Polish was the dominant language spoken at home. Frank was a gentle, quiet person, who was very close to his mother, and also, as mentioned, to Al Garshowitz, with whom he played semi-pro American football with the Eastwood Lions before enlisting in the RCAF, having worked briefly for Otis, the elevator manufacturers.

Donald Hopkinson was born at Royton, Oldham, in Lancashire in September 1920 as a second child. Just four months later his mother died of cancer, and Donald went to live with his grandfather, and an aunt, uncle and cousin. After his father remarried, a half brother and two half sisters were added to his family. A keen cricketer, Donald attended grammar school in Royton, before working in the office of the local Co-operative Society. He enlisted in the RAF in December 1941.

Richard Bolitho was born in Portrush, County Antrim, in January 1920, but was brought to England early on by his parents, who kept a hotel in Nottingham. Richard eventually moved in with his aunt, who ran a grocery shop in Kimberley, but after her death, his father sold the hotel and took over the shop. After attending school in nearby Heanor, Don worked for Ericcsons Telephones at Beeston, and enlisted in the RAF in November 1940.

The final member of the crew, flight engineer John Kinnear, did not become involved with Astell and the others until they had already carried out four operations with 57 Squadron. He was born in Fife, Scotland, in November 1921, and grew up to be a likeable, carefree young man who was mad about flying. He worked as a mechanic until he was old enough to enlist, and this he did in 1939. He was at 1654 Conversion Unit at the same time as the other members of his future crew, but does not appear to have arrived at 57 Squadron until later. He flew his first operations with the crew against Hamburg on the night of 3/4 March 1943 and Essen two nights later.

Astell wrote home for the last time on 14 May, and although tension must have been growing at Scampton, he took pains to keep any hint of it from his family. He enclosed a copy of his will, joking that the RAF takes on some funny ideas in telling all squadron members to make one. He closed by saying, 'There is no news at all from here. Lovely weather and a very quiet life'. Astell's will was witnessed by Henry Maudslay and Norm

Barlow, and fate would decree that the lives of these three men and their crews would end within a few miles of each other in the flatlands of rural Germany between the Ruhr and the Dutch frontier a few days hence.

Astell took off from Scampton at 21.59 along with S/L Henry Maudslay and P/O Les Knight as the final section of wave one. The three Lancasters remained in loose formation across the North Sea, heading for the gap between the islands of Schouwen and Walcheren in the Scheldt Estuary. All apparently proceeded according to plan until shortly after they crossed into Germany. As Maudslay and Knight made a course alteration, Astell continued on the original heading. It was only a brief parting of the ways and Astell soon found the correct track. He followed hard on the heels of his colleagues, perhaps a minute behind, two at the most. It is important to establish that Astell's deviation from track was not responsible in itself for the crash a few minutes later.

Eyewitnesses were awoken by the sound of two aircraft thundering over their rooftops. By the time they had got up and gone outside to investigate, Astell was upon them, colliding with an electricity pylon. This proves that Astell was following the same heading as the others and was at about the same altitude. After hitting the pylon, the Lancaster erupted in flames, scraped over the farmhouse and crashed a few seconds later in the field behind the neighbouring farmhouse. The bomb did not explode on contact, but rolled into the field, on fire, for about a hundred yards before it detonated. Perhaps the attention of Astell and his crew was focused ahead, searching in the distance for the telltale glow of exhausts from the other Lancasters, and this was the reason that they failed to spot a hazard to aircraft while they were flying at the ultra low level that had been discussed at the pre-operational briefing. We will, of course, never know the real reason. The incident took place at about 00.15 DBST, and ED864 was the third of the nineteen Lancasters of Operation *Chastise* to be lost before any of the targets had been reached. The pylon struck by Astell was repaired and remains to this day where it stood in 1943.

The wreckage of Astell's Lancaster lies in a field behind the Lammers' farm house. The charred remains of a crew member in the foreground provides a stark and poignant image of war.

## Tour Guide

In 2001 I spent a few days with Andreas and his lovely family at their home in Oer-Erkenschwick on the edge of the Ruhr near Recklinghausen. We travelled to the town of Raesfeld, where we met up with Richard Sühling and his wife Margret. Richard is a local historian, and he is a principal curator of the small local museum, in which the crash of Astell's Lancaster is documented. Richard took us to the crash site in a field a short distance from Raesfeld near Marbeck. We talked to *Frau* Lammers, behind whose farmhouse the field is situated, and whose father was the *Herr* Tücking who witnessed the crash and its aftermath. Her son and daughter-in-law now run the farm. We photographed the scene from every angle and ascertained the line of flight up to the impact with the pylon in order to understand as clearly as possible the cause of the loss. We have since visited the site on a number of occasions, and in September 2005 I took Heather Wareing, the sister of F/L

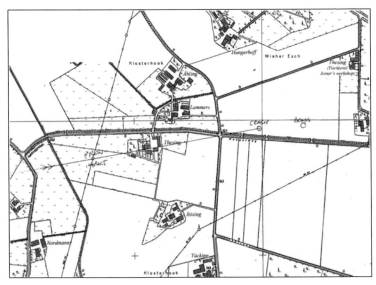

A map of Astell's crash site indicating the direction of flight, the pylon, the crash site and the approximate place where the bomb exploded.

The castle at Raesfeld.

Astell, to visit the crash site. She had not seen it before, and last visited his grave at Reichswald in 1955, when, coincidentally, she was stationed at the Möhne Lake, her brother's intended destination on the night he died, while she was employed as a civil servant.

On a previous visit I had asked Richard Sühling about the possibility of a permanent memorial to Astell and his crew at the crash site. I am happy to state that on Sunday 20 November 2005 a ceremony took place to dedicate a granite stone with plaque, which stands at the edge of the field within feet of where ED864 came down. We are grateful to Richard, Margret, Reinhard Niessing and the other members of the Raesfeld Heimat Verein for organising and financing the project, to big Guido (the stonemason) and to Herr Lammers, to whom the field belongs, for his unreserved willingness to accommodate the memorial. This is the only Dams operation crash site still to yield fragments of wreckage. Depending on the season and condition of the field, which is used to grow corn, it is possible to find tiny pieces of aluminium, .303 rounds and casings and

Richard and Margret Sühling in the Raesfeld Museum.

Entrance to the museum at Raesfeld.

Astell's pylon near Marbeck.

The Thesing farmhouse near Astell's crash site.

The wayside statue in its post war location.

Richard Sühling at Astell's crash site.

A view along the axis of Astell's crash.

The dedication of the memorial stone at Astell's crash site.

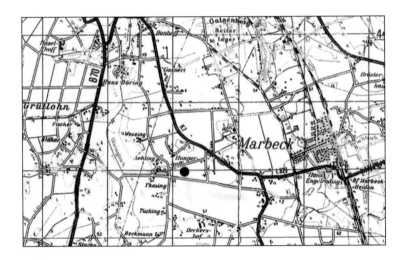

slivers of Perspex, particularly after ploughing. However, it is necessary to respect the fact that the field is part of a working farm, and courtesy would suggest permission be sought at the house before trampling the land.

From Oberhausen or Gelsenkirchen we travel along the A2 (E34) as far as the Bottrop junction. Here we pick up the A31 in the direction of Gronau. We follow the A31 until exit 37 for Schermbeck. At the junction with the B58 we turn left towards the towns of Haltern and Raesfeld. We travel a short distance until meeting a major crossroads with traffic lights. We take a left onto the B224 and head for Raesfeld. We then follow the B224 into the centre of Raesfeld, where we join the B70 for Borken. We leave Raesfeld behind us and travel along a tree-lined rural stretch of the B70 still heading towards Borken. After we have travelled for a few minutes, and just after crossing the Döringbach (a small stream), to the right we see a farmhouse, and directly thereafter a narrow right-hand turn. We take that road as far as the first fork, where we bear left. Continue to the next fork and keep right. Continue, going over a crossroads, and eventually the road bends to the left heading due north. Shortly thereafter the Tücking farm appears on the left-hand side. We maintain our course, ignoring a road branching off to the right. We are now on narrow single-track roads linking the neighbouring farms. At the next crossroads we are at our destination. Immediately to our left is the Lammers' farmhouse and yard, and over our left shoulder the neighbouring Thesing house. Looking over the Thesing's roof we can see the top of the pylon struck by Astell's Lancaster. Turning right at this crossroads we have the crash site in the field on our left behind a high hedge. Maybe fifty or so metres further on is a gap in the hedge and a rampart across the ditch. Here you will find the stone and plaque mentioned above erected as a permanent memorial to F/L Astell and his crew who perished in this spot.

CHAPTER 4

# F/L R.N.G. Barlow
## ED927, AJ-E
## Haldern-Herken, North of Rees

## Dams Raid

F/L Barlow, an Australian from Melbourne, was a graduate of
the Commonwealth Air Training Plan, and began a tour with 61
Squadron in the autumn of 1942. At almost 32 years of age he
was one of a number of more senior pilots to be posted to 617
Squadron. Having brought a badly damaged Lancaster home on
more than one occasion, 'Norm' Barlow had become regarded as
a press-on type. At least two of his crew, flight engineer, Sgt Sam
Whillis, and bomb-aimer, Sgt Alan Gillespie, came to Scampton
with him, and the other members of his Dams crew were also
recruited from 61 Squadron. His wireless operator, F/O
Williams, was another of the over thirty brigade, having been
born in Queensland, Australia, in 1909. He hoped to be retained
by 61 Squadron as a non-flying signals officer at the conclusion
of his tour, now just two trips away, and there is a suggestion
that he and other members of this crew were 'sold' on the move
to 617 Squadron, on the basis of doing just one more operation
rather than two.

Barlow had the honour of opening the proceedings for

Operation *Chastise* by being the first to take off at 21.28 hours on a clear, bright evening. This honour should have fallen to Joe McCarthy, but his beloved Q-Queenie sprang a glycol leak at start up, and by the time he had transferred to the spare aircraft and sorted out an errant compass deviation card, it was a fraction after 22.00 hours before he finally raced across the grass track to play his part in the operation. Although labelled wave two, the five aircraft of this section bound for the Sorpe Dam, captained by Barlow, Munro, Byers, Rice and McCarthy, preceded wave one into the air. This was by virtue of their longer journey to the enemy coast via the Frisian Islands, which they hoped to cross as wave one did likewise much further south. Had circumstances not so dictated, six aircraft would have had the Sorpe as their primary target, but F/L Wilson was absent, because of illness, although there were only nineteen available aircraft for the twenty-one crews who had trained anyway.

With McCarthy trailing behind and desperately trying to make up time, the others made their way across the North Sea at around fifty feet, not in formation, but mostly within visual range of each other. Barlow would probably have observed the loss of Byers just beyond the island of Vlieland, and may have seen Rice

Barlow's *Upkeep* being kept company by the local mayor, who, at the time, believed it to be a fuel tank.

bounce off the water, thus ending his involvement in the operation.

We know nothing of Barlow's passage along a south-easterly heading across Holland, but shortly after turning east and crossing into Germany he suffered an identical fate to that which killed Astell and his crew. High-tension cables, supported by tall pylons, hung like a spider's web across the Lancaster's path, and Barlow had the misfortune to fly into one. The aircraft ploughed into a field a few hundred yards further on, where it burned furiously. The bomb did not detonate, and it was recovered by the German military, who quickly uncovered its secrets. The time was recorded as 23.50 DBST, and there were no survivors from this, the second aircraft to go down. Since 1943 the surface of the field has risen by about ten feet and there are no fragments left to find.

## Tour Guide

In May 2001 I made my first visit to Rees, to the place where F/L Barlow and his crew died. Andreas and Horst had been there a few months earlier, and with the aid of Horst's metal detector had found three small pieces of aluminium. These fragments, Andreas believes, were the very last to remain in the ground. As we wandered about taking photographs, the farmer drove out to us to ask what we were doing on his land. His initial reserve soon disappeared as Andreas explained our presence and talked about the Dams Raid, of which *Herr* Hegmann knew nothing, despite being born in 1943. He did know of the crash through his father, however, and described a substantial piece of wreckage, which he was using to cover the access hole to a sewage pit in his farm-yard. This was the time of the foot and mouth outbreak in the UK, and he was paranoid about the infection crossing over to Germany. We were invited back to examine the artefact when the scare was over. A year later we returned, and purchased the large steel plate from the crash for fifty Euros.

We proceed along the A3 (E35) in the direction of the Dutch border until reaching exit 4 (Rees). The slip road brings us to a junction with the B67, where we turn right towards Rees. We continue to the next major crossroads, where we turn left onto the L459 towards Haldern. Maintaining our course we see on

Barlow's crash site with pylons on the horizon.

Barlow's crash site second field and pond.

The Sorpe Lake with dam off to the left.

The Sorpe Dam dry side and compensating basin.

Sorpe Dam from the overflow channel.

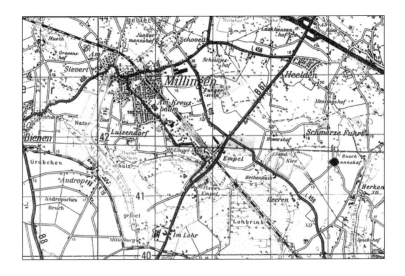

our left a dredging operation featuring a lake, and a little further on to our right some houses and farms. We look out now for a narrow left-hand turn, which takes us onto a single-track tarmac road. Continuing along here we come across, but ignore, a track branching off to the left. The significance of this track is that it marks the start of the field in which F/L Barlow's Lancaster crashed. Continue until the road branches left and right at the end of the field. The wreckage came to rest in this right-hand corner, although in May 1943 the level was two or three metres lower than now. Then, the field, and the one on the other side of the track containing the small pond, were linked by a tunnel, under which cattle could pass. After the war the authorities removed all trace of the Lancaster, to the extent that it took an intensive search in 2001 to uncover two or three small pieces. Standing with one's back to the pond one can see at the far end of the field the line of high-tension cables responsible for the demise of Barlow and his crew.

CHAPTER 5

# P/O L.J. Burpee
## ED865, AJ-S
## On the Former Night Fighter Station
## at Gilze-Rijen

### Dams Raid

Lewis Burpee was born in Ottawa in March 1918, and gained a
university degree before enlisting in the RCAF in December
1940. He arrived in England in late 1941, and began his first tour
with 106 Squadron in October 1942. He flew his first operation
as second pilot to a F/S Stan Jones on 15 October when Cologne
was the target, and a week later accompanied the same crew to
Genoa. He captained his own crew on an operation for the first
time on 7 November, but was forced to abandon the trip, which
was again to Genoa, when his navigator became ill. Between
then and leaving 106 Squadron he flew a further twenty-six
times, notching up in the process five more early returns. As far
as Burpee's Dams crew is concerned, his flight engineer Guy
Pegler and rear gunner Joe Brady were with him from the start
of his tour, while mid-upper gunner Bill Long joined on 9
January, navigator Tom Jaye on 21 January, wireless operator
Len Weller on 16 February, and bomb-aimer Jack Arthur arrived

in time for their last operation, against Essen on 12/13 March.

Burpee and his crew were part of the third and final wave of Operation *Chastise*, along with Ottley, Townsend, Brown and Anderson. Had an aircraft been available, or, as we are told, had crew sickness not intervened, Divall's name would also have been included. These crews were to act as a mobile reserve, remaining at Scampton until a clear picture had emerged of events in enemy territory. As it turned out, it was some two hours after the departure of McCarthy that the third wave took off, each flying independently via the southerly route, as travelled by the first wave, to await instructions from Grantham. Burpee was the second away at 00.11 hours, and we know he arrived safely at the Dutch coast and headed for the narrow gap between the night fighter airfields at Eindhoven and Gilze-Rijen. There is no question that the defences had been alerted by the passage of the first two waves through Holland, and both Burpee and Brown following him were forced to take evasive action to avoid the searchlights and flak. Brown witnessed Burpee's end, describing the Lancaster as on fire, before crashing onto the aerodrome at

Burpee and crew. He is 3rd from the right.

The Sorpe Dam.

The road atop the Sorpe Dam with the village of Langscheid
ahead.

Beautiful scenery surrounding the Sorpe Reservoir.

A model of Gilze-Rijen airfield on display in the base's
museum, showing it as it was at the time of Burpee's crash.

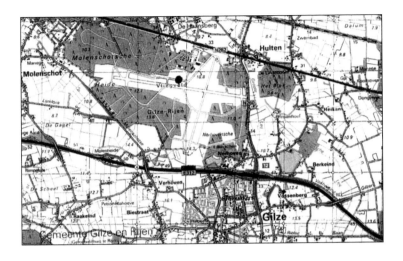

Gilze-Rijen, where the Upkeep weapon exploded like a rising sun causing massive damage to buildings and equipment.

## Tour Guide

It is not possible to access the precise location of Burpee's crash site, but we can get close. As stated, the Lancaster came down on the airfield at Gilze-Rijen, and at the time of writing it is in use by the Dutch Air Force as an operational base. It is therefore a restricted area and not accessible to the general public. Approaching from the direction of Eindhoven on the A58 (E312), we travel past Tilburg heading for Breda. We leave the A58 (E312) at Junction 12 (Gilze), and turn right onto the N260 in the direction of Hulten. We remain on the N260 and very soon have the former night fighter airfield of Gilze-Rijen on our left.

CHAPTER 6

# P/O V.W. Byers
## ED934, AJ-K
## In the Sea off Texel/Vlieland

### Dams Raid

P/O Byers, like Burpee, a Canadian, came from 467 Squadron, RAAF, and was yet another mature man, having attained the age of thirty-two . He was already thirty when he joined the RCAF, and was probably close to the upper age limit for new recruits. He arrived at 467 Squadron from 1654 Conversion Unit on 5 February 1943, along with two of his Dams crew, flight engineer Sgt Taylor, and wireless operator Sgt Wilkinson. While at 1654 Conversion Unit he flew on four occasions with 'Mick' Martin, who was instructing there at the time. It seems that Byers filled the remaining crew positions with spare bods who had been at 467 Squadron since November 1942. By the time of Byer's posting to 617 Squadron he had managed to get four operations under his belt, including a mining sortie, a trip to Stuttgart with an unserviceable rear turret and a raid on St Nazaire.

Byers took off from Scampton at 21.30 hours as the third member of wave two. The route was supposed to take them over the lightly defended island of Vlieland, but in the twilight conditions it would have been difficult to distinguish the profile of the island from its southerly neighbour, Texel. It should also be said that the gap between Texel and Den Helder on the Dutch mainland would have looked similar, and could have been mistaken for that between Vlieland and Texel. We do know that the wind from the north was a little stronger than forecast, and that both the first and second waves were blown south of the intended track. This almost resulted in disaster as Gibson found himself over the heavily defended island of Walcheren in the Scheldt Estuary, rather than in the gap between it and Schouwen to the north. As Byers approached Vlieland he climbed to get his bearings, thus suggesting that he was not absolutely certain of them. He passed safely over the island at about four hundred feet, and was over the sea again when a heavy flak shell found him. Other crews watched the Lancaster catch fire and fall into the sea east of Vlieland.

Although it seems certain that Byers was hit by flak from the southern tip of Vlieland and crashed in the sea on the eastern side of the island, some Dutch fishermen believe that the incident actually occurred much further south between the southern tip of Texel and Den Helder on the Dutch mainland. For that to be the case it would have been necessary for the other

Marine flak installations on Texel.

Lancasters of the second wave to be also substantially off course, because a number of crewmembers in these aircraft witnessed the end of Byers and his crew. That said, and as already suggested, the profile of the islands of Vlieland and Texel and that of Texel and Den Helder would have appeared similar at low level in twilight. Clearly one cannot visit a crash site in the sea, but one can view the approximate location, or in this case, possible locations.

## Tour Guide

We follow the Dutch coast road, which takes us all the way up to Den Helder. From here Texel is clearly visible, and I recommend you take the short ferry ride across to the island. In so doing you will cross the Molengat, where Byers would have come down if the fishermen were correct. The strong current of the Marsdiep has gouged out a deep channel from the southern rim of Texel as the tide between the island and the mainland ebbs and flows, and anything coming down there would be carried towards the

Texel scene.

Texel scene.

northern coast of Holland. This could account for the location of the one recovered body from the Lancaster, which was found much further north off Harlingen. Once on Texel drive to its northern end, and look across to the north-east, to where I believe the crash occurred. The body of F/Sgt McDowell lies in the General Cemetery at Harlingen.

# CHAPTER 7

# P/O W.G. Divall
## JA874, KC-E
## Steinbeck, Near Recke

### Dortmund-Ems Canal Raid

P/O George Divall was born in Surrey in 1922, and like many of the wartime influx of pilots he was sent to Canada in 1941 for basic training. He arrived at Scampton in February 1943 to undertake his first operational tour with 57 Squadron, and was, therefore, still relatively inexperienced when he and his crew were posted to 617 Squadron on 10 April as a late replacement for a crew dismissed by Gibson supposedly for not achieving the required standard. This allowed him only a fraction over one month to train for Operation *Chastise*, compared with the six weeks available to most of the others, many of whom were seasoned campaigners, and this would have placed him at a distinct disadvantage. In the event, Divall and his crew did not take part, ostensibly through illness, although there was a shortage of serviceable aircraft on the night anyway. It was, in fact, not until July that he undertook his first sorties with 617 Squadron, the first an attack on an electrical transformer station at San Polo d'Enza on 15/16 July, followed by Leghorn docks on the way home on 24/25 July, having spent the intervening

# P/O W.G. Divall

Looking westwards along the stretch of the Mittelland Canal
near Steinbeck, where Divall crashed.

period at Blida in North Africa. He was in action again on 29/30
July for a leafleting operation to Milan in another shuttle
operation involving a stopover in North Africa. The Dortmund-
Ems Canal operation was only his fourth in five months at 617
Squadron. On this night he was the last away from Coningsby,
at around 00.04 hours, as part of the second wave led by acting
S/L Allsebrook.

The Divall crew would have experienced the same difficulties
as the others in the conditions of poor visibility, particularly with
regard to accurate navigation, and this probably led to the second
wave reaching the target area about ten miles north of the briefed
location south-west of Ladbergen. We know this from Shannon's
post-raid report, and it appears that he was the only one of
Allsebrook's section to realise the error and search successfully
for the genuine aiming point. Divall was actually searching an
area to the north-east of Ladbergen, where the Mittelland Canal
runs east to west before turning south to meet with the
Dortmund-Ems Canal in the Wet Triangle at Bergeshövede. A
witness at Steinbeck, a village on the southern bank of the
Mittelland Canal, heard an aircraft fly to and fro between Achmer

in the east and Bergeshövede. Eventually it approached her parent's farmhouse, flying east to west and parallel with the waterway on its northern side, apparently on fire. The 12,000-lb bomb was dropped onto the northern bank a few hundred yards before the farmhouse was reached, where it exploded, and the Lancaster ploughed in a second or two later almost opposite the house. Most of the wreckage fell into the canal, but the rear turret with its occupant was catapulted to within a dozen or so yards of the rear of the house.

## Tour Guide

It was late afternoon on a beautiful sunny day in May 2002 when Andreas and I set off on the relatively short journey from Bergeshövede to Steinbeck near the town of Recke on the bank of the Mittelland Canal. We were going to the spot where Divall and his crew came down, and like many of the sites we had visited over the previous twelve months, it is unlikely that anyone had attempted to uncover the details in the years since the events took place. Andreas had been told by a local historian, Paul Nössler,

The gap in the trees on the northern bank where Divall crashed.

The gap in the trees on the northern bank where Divall crashed.

that the site would be clearly visible by the gaps in the trees on the canal bank, signifying the explosion of the bomb and the crash of the Lancaster. Sure enough, as we drove off the main road onto a narrow track by the Kälberberg Bridge, we could see the places. Some distance ahead near the Bad Bridge was a farm and houses, and we decided to call in at the farmhouse to see if anyone knew of an eyewitness. Andreas has an uncanny knack of finding at the first time of asking the one person in the world who has the information we are seeking, and as we drove into the farmyard and parked up, a man appeared from one of the buildings. He and Andreas disappeared for about ten minutes, and when Andreas returned, he did so with a lady who had witnessed some of the events of Divall's crash fifty-nine years earlier as a ten-year-old. The friendliness and willingness of *Frau* Brönstrup to help complete strangers was remarkable, and while passing on details of her experience on that night, she took us into the back garden to point out the spot where the rear turret came to rest. When we left her we walked along both banks of the canal to get our bearings and try to picture the course of events.

Travelling from the direction of Osnabrück along the A30

Frau Brönstrup's farmhouse, and the spot beyond the fence where the rear turret came to rest.

Andreas on the northern bank at the site of Divall's crash.

The southern bank from Divall's crash site.

Divall's crash site.

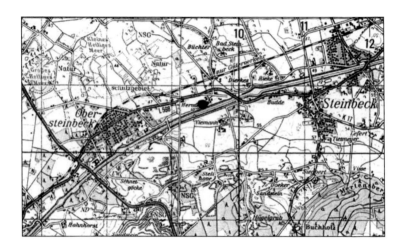

(E30) towards the Dutch border, we leave the motorway at
Junction 10 (Hörstel), and turn left onto the K38 heading
towards Hörstel. At the T-junction with the L501 we turn right
and continue over the Mittelland Canal until reaching a crossroads. Here we turn left onto the L598 and head towards
Obersteinbeck/Hopsten. We remain on the L598 for some time,
crossing back onto the northern bank of the Mittelland Canal
and ultimately passing through the little town of Obersteinbeck.
After Obersteinbeck the road yet again carries us over the
Mittelland Canal onto its southern bank. Immediately thereafter, we park the vehicle and walk back onto the bridge.
Looking towards the west along the length of the Canal we see
another bridge. Shortly before the far bridge, on the right hand
or northern bank, a gap in the trees shows where Divall's
Lancaster crashed. Opposite, and set back, is a farmhouse and
the field onto which the rear turret came to rest. Much closer to
where we are standing, also on the right-hand bank, is another
gap in the trees where Divall's 12,000-pounder exploded. A
towpath on both banks allows access for pedestrians.

# CHAPTER 8

# W/C G.W. Holden
## EE144, KC-S
## Nordhorn

## Dortmund-Ems Canal Raid

S/L George Holden, late of 4 Group, arrived at Scampton on 2 July 1943 to take up his duty as senior flight commander and squadron commander elect of 617 Squadron. In April Holden had completed six months as an acting Wing Commander in command of 102 Squadron, 'Dinghy' Young's old unit. On 1 July, he flew to Scampton in an Anson, but his logbook does not state whether or not he landed. He may simply have been taking a look from the air at his new home, before his posting there on the following day. It would be a further month before Gibson departed the squadron, and Holden needed time to learn the ways of the Lancaster, a type unfamiliar to him and to all others whose careers had been spent in 4 Group.

Holden was a 4 Group man to the core, and perhaps not an obvious choice to replace the charismatic Gibson, now the most celebrated squadron commander in the entire service. His selection actually began a trend of appointing 4 Group men to the position, such as Cheshire, Tait and Fauquier, men who would carry the squadron through to the end of the bombing war in late

April 1945. If Harris, and one might reasonably assume some involvement on his part, was prepared to look outside of 5 Group for Gibson's successor, why did he sanction the appointment of Holden from among the wealth of qualified existing squadron commanders available? It has to be said, that there was something of the Gibson character in Holden. His career to this point had been distinguished, and he had been involved in some unusual and spectacular operations. He had also rubbed shoulders with some of the Command's finest young bloods, many of whom were gathered within the squadrons of 4 Group, and were themselves seen as shining lights. Not all had survived to the summer of 1943, and of those who had (whose operational careers had begun in 1940), Holden was unquestionably among the brightest prospects. If Dinghy Young (a 4 Group contemporary of Holden and Cheshire) had survived (see Chapter 14), or perhaps even Henry Maudslay from the 'class of 41' (see Chapter 11), then they would also undoubtedly have been in the frame, but they were gone. Cheshire had progressed to the rank of Group Captain, which generally speaking at that time, precluded him from the command of a squadron. This latter restriction was in the process of being revised, however, as Pathfinder squadrons were now being led by Group Captains, with Wing Commanders filling the roll of flight commander.

Holden began basic training, presumably part time as a reservist, in May 1937. On 1 September 1939, the day German forces began their assault on Poland, he joined 9 Flying Training School at Hullavington, moved on to Benson between January and early May 1940, and thence to 10 Operational Training Unit (OTU) at Abingdon, where he learned to fly Whitleys. This was the type operated by 4 Group until the advent of the Halifax, and it would be the spring of 1942 before it was finally withdrawn from operational service with the Command. He passed out as a first pilot, day only, with an average rating on 18 September, and immediately joined 78 Squadron at Dishforth. Here, he began working up to operational status, and undertook his first sortie as second pilot to F/L Pattison in a raid on Antwerp on the night of 26/27 September. His second sortie was to Amsterdam with his flight commander, S/L Wildey, who would eventually take command of 10 Squadron, and lose his life in action in October 1942, the same month in which Holden would gain his first command. Finally, on 11 November, Holden was signed out as a fully qualified Whitley captain by the newly appointed commanding officer, W/C 'Charles' Whitworth. Two nights later he undertook his first operation as crew captain, his eighth sortie in all, but like many others operating in poor weather conditions that night, he was forced to abandon his sortie and return home. He put matters right on 15/16 November, however, when participating in an unusually effective raid on Hamburg.

Late in 1940, Prime Minister Churchill pressed for the formation of a paratroop unit, as the forerunner of an airborne force for use in a future invasion of Europe. Plans were put in hand to carry out a special operation under the codename *Colossus*, with the purpose of ascertaining the viability of such an undertaking. Volunteers were brought together as X-Troop No. 11 SAS Battalion for an attack on an aqueduct over the River Tragino in Italy to be launched from Malta. Two aircraft were to carry out a diversionary bombing attack on marshalling yards at nearby Foggia, while six others delivered the parachutists into position. Nos 51 and 78 Squadrons were each selected to provide four aircraft and crews under the command of W/C James Tait, who had recently begun a short spell as commanding officer of the former. Among the pilots from 78 Squadron was P/O Holden, who flew with Tait on a container-dropping test as part of the run-up on 2 February. On completion of their task the surviving commandos were to gather at a point on the coast for evacuation by submarine. The force departed for Malta on the night of 7/8 February, and carried out the operation on 10/11 February. In the event, not all of the commandos were dropped within range of their target, and if this were not unfortunate enough, one of the diversionary Whitleys had to be abandoned in the area selected for the ground force's withdrawal, thus alerting the local defenders. Some damage was inflicted upon the aqueduct, but all of the soldiers were captured on their way to the *rendezvous*, and they were joined soon afterwards by the Whitley crew.

This operation was Holden's twentieth, and his last with 78 Squadron, which he left with an above average rating to join 35 Squadron at Linton-on-Ouse. No. 35 Squadron had been reformed at Boscombe Down in November 1940 to introduce the Halifax into operational service, and was attracting the leading bomber pilots in 4 Group. Holden arrived on 25 February 1941, and met up again with Tait, who had now reverted to Squadron Leader rank and was a flight commander under the portly personage of the squadron commander, W/C R.W.P. Collings, another of the Command's great characters. The Halifax suffered many teething problems, and the demand for modifications ensured only a trickle of new aircraft from the factories. As a result, following its operational baptism in March, the type operated only intermittently and in very small numbers for some time.

Holden flew his first Halifax sortie against Duisburg on 11/12 June, and over the ensuing five weeks managed ten more. A major assault on the German cruisers *Scharnhorst*, *Gneisenau* and *Prinz Eugen* at Brest, the first two-named having been in residence there since the end of March, was planned for 24 July. The operation was to be undertaken in daylight by Halifaxes accompanied by 1 and 3 Group Wellingtons, and under extensive diversionary activity and a heavy fighter escort. It was discovered at the eleventh hour, however, that the *Scharnhorst* had slipped away to La Pallice, some two hundred miles further south, and it was decided to send the Halifax element after her, while the remainder of the original plan went ahead at Brest. Fifteen Halifaxes from 35 and 76 Squadrons duly attacked the *Scharnhorst*, causing extensive damage, but lost five of their number in the process, and all of the surviving aircraft sustained damage to some degree. Holden was forced to bring his bombs home after flak shot away the electrical release gear. One of his crew was killed, while two others were wounded, one seriously. Holden's flight commander at the time was S/L Jimmy Marks, one of the brightest stars in Bomber Command. Marks would gain command of 35 Squadron in 1942, only to lose his life in action shortly after taking the Squadron into the Pathfinder Force as one of the founder units.

Holden concluded his tour with a total of thirty-two operations, and was posted to the Heavy Conversion Flight at Linton-on-Ouse on 18 August. Here he remained until December, when he was detached to Upavon, before progressing to Marston Moor, Leeming and Pocklington in the role of instructor. At Pocklington, and now with the rank of Squadron Leader, he was put in charge of the Conversion Flight of 405 Squadron, a Canadian unit commanded by W/C Johnny Fauquier. While there, Holden flew on the second thousand bomber raid against Essen on 1/2 June 1942, and the third and final one on Bremen on 25/26 June, his thirty-third and thirty-fourth sorties. In July he was posted to 158 Squadron's Conversion Flight at East Moor, where he remained until 25 October. In the early hours of the previous day, 102 Squadron's commanding officer, W/C Bintley, had been killed in a freak accident on the runway at Holme-on-Spalding-Moor on return from Genoa, when another Halifax had crushed his cockpit on landing. Holden was posted as his replacement on 25th, and began a successful period of command, during which he operated a further eleven times, bringing his tally to forty-five. He was rested again on 20 April 1943, and thereafter seemed to kick his heels somewhat until the call came through from 617 Squadron. On 4 July, two days after his arrival at Scampton, he was taken up by Martin in EE148 for a local familiarisation trip, and the two paired up again on the following two days. On 7 July Holden flew with Gibson's Dams crew for the first time. W/C Holden was confirmed as the new commanding officer on 2 August, Gibson's final day on the squadron. The pair enjoyed a 1 hour 25 minute farewell cross-country flight together in ED933 with Gibson's crew, soon to be Holden's crew, in attendance.

A commanding officer's crew possessed a certain status, despite the fact that Gibson's was a disparate bunch who had come together for the first time at Scampton, and had thus far completed only the Dams operation as the crew of the CO. Two of them, 'Terry' Taerum, a Canadian, and Fred 'Spam' Spafford from Australia, arrived via the 50 Squadron academy and 1654 Conversion Unit, while the wireless operator, Bob Hutchison, was well known to Gibson, having completed a tour with 106 Squadron. The front gunner, George Deering, whom Gibson described in *Enemy Coast Ahead* as green, had actually completed a first tour, and Operation *Chastise* would be his thirty-sixth sortie. His previous operations had been undertaken on Wellingtons with 1 Group's 103 Squadron, which he joined from 21 OTU on 16 August 1941. After screening he went to 22 OTU, on 11 May 1942, and took part in one or more of the thousand bomber raids. Of the other members of Gibson's Dams crew, flight engineer John Pulford remained with the squadron until losing his life in a Lancaster crash in February 1944, and the rear gunner, Richard Trevor-Roper, was eventually posted to the

Pathfinder's 97 Squadron, and was killed in action during the catastrophic Nuremberg raid at the end of March 1944. As a replacement for Pulford, Holden chose Dennis Powell, who had flown to the dams with Townsend. For the Dortmund-Ems Canal operation each Lancaster would carry an eight-man crew, so that each turret could be manned. To facilitate this a number of gunners were temporarily posted in from training units. The two final members of Holden's crew, the mid-upper and rear gunners, were respectively F/O Pringle and P/O Meikle.

Holden took off from Coningsby at 23.56 hours at the head of the first wave. Following in his prop wash were Martin, Knight and Wilson They remained in close contact until reaching the

Guy Gibson at the time of handing command of 617 Squadron to W/C George Holden. In the picture also are the members of Gibson's Dams crew, four of whom died with Holden at Nordhorn on their way to the Dortmund-Ems Canal. 3rd from left Taerum, 4th from left Deering, 6th from left Hutchison. 9th from left Holden and 11th from left Spafford. 5th from left is Trevor-roper, who was Gibson's rear gunner for Operation Chastise. He died in a Pathfinder Lancaster of 97 Squadron during the infamous Nuremberg raid of the 30/31st of March 1944, when 95 heavy bombers failed to return. Gibson is 7th from the left, while 10th is Pulford, Gibson's much maligned flight engineer, who was killed in Bill Suggitt's Lancaster during a transit flight in February 1944.

George Holden's crash site at Nordhorn.

town of Nordhorn, some twenty miles or seven minutes' flying time from the *rendezvous* point at Wettringen. In their path stood a church, and Holden elected to climb over it rather than go round. This was probably an instinctive decision taken by a man who had spent his extensive operational career believing that H-E-I-G-H-T spelt safety. In contrast, for those who had been at 617 Squadron since the start, low flying had become a way of life. Martin, Knight and Wilson instinctively remained at rooftop height and simply changed course to miss the church. Holden's decision to climb to perhaps 300 feet presented his aircraft in profile to a lone light-flak gun on a factory roof over to starboard. Only a few shells were fired, but at least one punctured a wing tank and set the Lancaster ablaze. Within seconds it had flipped over and nosed into the ground about half a mile from the town centre. The fiercely burning wreckage lay only yards from a farmhouse containing *Herr* and *Frau* Hood and six of their children. The youngsters were sheltering in the cellar, and the parents ventured up into the house to collect night-clothes. It was then, after some fifteen minutes' of cooking in the blazing wreckage, that the bomb went up, flattening the house and all of the other buildings in the farmyard. Somehow *Herr* Hood survived, but the remains of his wife were found under the rubble when daylight came. She proved to be the only German fatality on a night of heavy loss for 617 Squadron. The explosion shattered windows and stripped tiles from roofs within a half-mile radius.

## Tour Guide

In May 2002 I made my first visit to Nordhorn, as always with Andreas as my guide, and on this occasion also with Horst. I wanted to see where the lives of George Holden and his crew ended. Just outside the town is the farm, which has been the home of *Herr* Hood for his entire life. He and his wife now live in a bungalow built within the farmyard, while their son and daughter-in-law occupy the farmhouse. *Herr* Hood was a six-year-old child when his mother was killed, but there was no

The spot where Holden crashed with four of Gibson's Dams crew.

Herr Hood, whose mother was the only German fatality.

trace of animosity, and we were made most welcome. The Hoods were interested to know something of the crew, and had the torn-out pages of Alan Cooper's book From the Dams to the *Tirpitz*, which dealt with Holden's crash. As *Herr* and *Frau* Hood senior speak no English, they were unable to read the text, and assumed from the photo of Shannon and Trevor-Roper that they were the men killed. They were amazed to find out that eight men had died on the edge of their land, and that those in the photo were not among them. They took us to the place where the Lancaster came down, which is separated from the farmyard by the width of a path. A lake was created in 1972, which takes in part of the crash site and covers most of the area between the farm and the town. Horst made a quick and fruitless survey with his metal detector, but we knew the creation of the lake would have obliterated any trace of the crash.

Travelling from the direction of Osnabrück we journey along the A30 (E30) towards the Dutch frontier. We leave the A30 (E30) at Junction 3 Nordhorn/Bad Bentheim. The slip road leads onto the B403. We turn left onto this road and head for

"a fruitless survey with a metal detector."

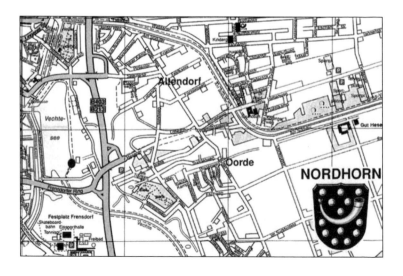

Nordhorn. Before Nordhorn the B403 and B213 merge as one under the name Osttangente. We remain on the Osttangente as far as the exit for the Frensdorfer Ring, in the direction of Nordhorn. We turn right onto the Frensdorfer Ring and cross back over Osttangente as if heading into Nordhorn. Now take the second exit on the right shortly after the flyover we have just passed, and this brings us onto a narrow road. We follow this road and take the first left. We park the car with the Vechta Lake in front of us at the point where a footpath leads us to the right. This brings us automatically past the farmhouse and yard of the Hood family. It was here that W/C Holden's Lancaster impacted the ground. When the bomb detonated it completely destroyed the house. The house we see today is a reconstruction.

# CHAPTER 9

# F/L J.V. Hopgood
## ED925, AJ-M
### Ostönnen, North-west of the Möhnesee

## Dams Raid

At the time of his death John Hopgood was a mere twenty-two years old, and yet something of a veteran. A Londoner, he had passed out as a pilot at Cranwell on 16 February 1941. A spell at 14 OTU at Cottesmore in Rutland followed, where F/L Nettleton checked him out for his Hampden solo. Nettleton, eleven months hence, would lead the epic daylight raid by elements of 44 and 97 Squadrons against the MAN diesel works at Augsburg, and be awarded the Victoria Cross as a result. In July 1941 Hopgood was posted to 50 Squadron to begin his operational career, and flew his first sortie to Bremen on 12 July as navigator to a F/O Abbott. The fighter-style single-seat cockpit of the Hampden precluded a second pilot's position, and it became standard practice for the navigator/bomb-aimer's role to be undertaken by a qualified pilot. After operating once more with F/O Abbott, Hopgood carried out eight more Hampden sorties as navigator/bomb-aimer to a P/O Smith, before being posted to 25 OTU at Finningley at the end of October. While still with 25 OTU he began converting to Manchesters at Bircotes, and it was here that he came into contact with P/O Whamond, one of the future mainstays of 106 Squadron. On 17 February 1942 Hopgood was signed off as a qualified Manchester pilot by W/C Lynch-Blosse, soon to be killed in action on his first sortie as commander of 44 (Rhodesia) Squadron. Hopgood was posted to Coningsby to join 106 Squadron, commanded at the time, as stated earlier, by W/C Allen. No. 106 Squadron was already recognised as one of 5 Group's finest units, and over the ensuing year its reputation would flourish under its new commander.

Hopgood's introduction to Manchester operations came as second pilot to Whamond on a mining sortie on 20 March, the day on which Gibson assumed command of the squadron. After two further operations as second pilot, he flew as captain of his own crew for the first time against Rostock on 23 April. No. 106 Squadron was among the last in 5 Group to take on the ill-fated Manchester, but, thankfully, the type was approaching the end of its short period of service, and in May it was replaced by the Lancaster. It was Hopgood who saw Gibson safely through his conversion onto the type. Hopgood's first two Lancaster sorties were the thousand bomber raids against Cologne and Essen on 30/31 May and 1/2 June respectively. The former was an outstanding success, while the latter was an abysmal failure, but Hopgood came through both with flying colours. The remainder of his tour served to demonstrate his abilities, and it established his reputation as a first-rate pilot and captain. His press-on spirit ensured his status as a member of Gibson's inner circle, and the bond between the two men would prove to be fateful. Hopgood concluded his tour with 106 Squadron in October 1942 with a total of forty-six operations to his credit, and he was awarded the DFC on the 27th. His next posting was to Station HQ Syerston in Nottinghamshire, where he carried out test flights in the new Hercules-powered Mk II Lancasters, and also instructed other pilots. This was followed by periods at the FIU at Ford and 1485 Bombing Gunnery Flight at Fulbeck, where he flew half a dozen different types on various duties. He was awarded a Bar to his DFC on 11 January 1943. This sojourn ended on 29 March, when he flew to Scampton, and officially joined the newly formed 617 Squadron under Gibson on the following day.

A Luftwaffe officer stands amidst the shattered remains of John Hopgood's Lancaster near the village of Ostönnen a few kilometres beyond the Möhne Dam. The photograph is reproduced with the kind permission of Helmut Euler, and appears also in his book, *Dambusters Through the Lense*

On 16 May John Hopgood took off with Gibson and Martin in a loose vic formation at 21.39 hours. He was entrusted with the responsibility of acting as Gibson's deputy at the Möhne Dam in the event of Gibson's loss. As it turned out, Gibson survived while Hopgood did not. As the first to attack, Gibson had the element of surprise on his side. The German gunners realised they were the object of attention, but until Gibson's Lancaster thundered towards them, they didn't know if they were simply a navigation pinpoint or the intended target. They certainly had no inkling of how the attack would be pressed forward and from which direction. Gibson provided them with all the answers, and when Hopgood (as the second to attack) began his fourteen-second run across the lake towards the centre of the dam at 00.33 hours, the gunners knew what to expect.

It wasn't the first time Hopgood had been fired upon that night. Flak batteries around Dülmen had scored hits, leaving the wireless operator, John Minchin, with a severe leg wound, while

Raid on the Ruhr whiskey being enjoyed on the Möhne Dam.

Hopgood sustained a facial injury, which required attention from Charles Brennan, the flight engineer. It seems likely that George Gregory in the front turret was mortally wounded also at this time. It is also believed that an engine was damaged, and this would prove to be critical during the aftermath of the attack. As Hopgood sped across the lake, the coloured tracer shells whipped into his face, and the crews circling nearby looked on in horror as a ribbon of flame stretched from an inboard engine back past the tail. They saw the bomb fall away too late and bounce over the parapet of the dam in the wake of the Lancaster. A huge detonation at the base of the dam reduced the powerhouse to rubble and sent a pall of smoke climbing into the air. Now Hopgood's only thought was to gain enough height to allow his crew to save themselves, but with only two good engines to haul the stricken Lancaster away from the valley floor, progress was slow.

Inside the fuselage a drama of life and death was being enacted. Jim Fraser knew he had dropped the bomb too late, but he had been distracted by the commotion caused by the fire. He

Hopgood's crash site.

The memorial at Hopgood's crash site.

The Möhne Dam

The village of Günne on the edge of the compensating basin.

A view from the dam across the Möhnesee.

Möhne Dam compensating basin.

The Möhne Dam  seen from the dry side.

Hopgood's grave at Rheinberg.

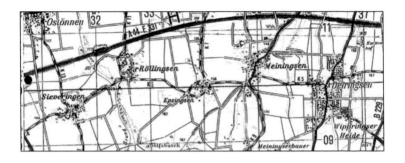

unpacked his parachute within the confines of his cramped compartment and tucked it under his arm. He opened the hatch in the floor, and saw with alarm the close proximity of the tree-tops. Unless the chute opened instantly he was a dead man. He knelt at the edge of the aperture and as he rolled forward he sensed the silk being snatched from his grasp by the slipstream. The tail wheel whistled past his head as he tumbled, and then the canopy filled with air and arrested his fall. After the briefest descent he felt the hard earth meet him.

Meanwhile, Tony Burcher had managed to extricate himself from the rear turret to reach his parachute. He was confronted with the sight of John Minchin crawling along the fuselage with a leg almost cut through. Burcher ensured his friend's parachute was firmly attached before pushing him through the rear door and holding onto the rip-chord. Sadly, it was in vain. Whether the gallant Minchin died as a result of his injuries or the fall is not known. Burcher strapped on his own chute and unpacked it as Fraser had done, then he plugged into the intercom to tell Hopgood he was leaving. Hopgood knew only seconds remained before the Lancaster tore itself apart, and he screamed at Burcher to get out. As the rear gunner stood in the doorway the aircraft was rent by an explosion as the fuel tank went up. Burcher was blasted into space and his back was hit a glancing blow by the tailplane. He landed heavily and was unable to walk, but he was alive. The shattered and burning remnants of the Lancaster fell out of the sky into a field at Ostönnen, six kilometres beyond the dam, and the bodies of Hopgood, Brennan, Earnshaw and Gregory were recovered by the Germans later that day.

# Tour Guide

To find the crash site we travel along the A44 (E331) from the direction of Dortmund towards Kassel until reaching exit 56 (Soest/Möhnesee). At the junction we turn left onto the B229 heading towards Delecke/Möhnesee. We follow this road until reaching a large crossroads, at which we will see a sign for the Bismarkturm. Here the B229 is intersected by the B516. We turn right onto the B516 towards Werl. We follow the B516 as far as a roundabout, which is an intersection with the L745. We turn right onto the L745 in the direction of Ostönnen. We follow this road until shortly before an underpass leading back beneath the A44 (E331). A narrow right-hand turn just before the underpass takes us to a track on the left. We leave the car at this point and go on foot along the track towards the nearby motorway. After a few metres we come across a wooden post bearing a brass plaque. This is the closest convenient point to the crash site of Hopgood's Lancaster, which, it is believed, fell approximately where the motorway now stands.

# CHAPTER 10

# F/L L.G. Knight
## JB144, KC-N
## Den Ham in Holland

## Dortmund-Ems Canal Raid

As future Dambuster 'Mick' Martin was preparing to leave 50 Squadron at the end of his first tour in September 1942, Sgt Les Knight arrived to start his. He was born in the Australian state of Victoria in 1921, and had the war not intervened, he would have become an accountant. With him from the training unit came five of his eventual Dams crew, only Ray Grayston, the flight engineer, being absent from the line-up, although he was already on the squadron. Knight's first operation with his new unit was against Wismar on Germany's Baltic coast on 1/2 October 1942, and it was not until his tenth, against Stuttgart on 22/23 November, that Grayston first flew with the crew in place of a Sgt Sunderland. It was at this time that Hopgood's future navigator, Ken Earnshaw, started to appear in the squadron records in the crew of a Sgt Schofield, and another 617 Squadron original, gunner F/O Richard Trevor-Roper, rejoined the squadron for a second tour.

Knight returned from Operation *Chastise* a hero. His attack on the Eder Dam with the first wave's last available bomb was

Les Knight and crew.

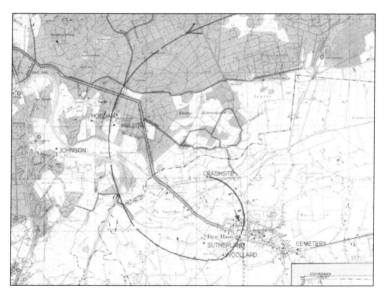

The path described by Knight's stricken Lancaster around Den Ham as his crew parachuted to safety. The flight path halts abruptly at the point where the aircraft hit treetops, lost flying speed and nosed into the ground taking the life of the pilot.

Les Knight's crash site at Den Ham in Holland.

absolutely copybook, despite the most testing requirements of airmanship. As he flew away elated by his success, he had the satisfaction of seeing the valley in full flood. The Dortmund-Ems Canal operation would prove to be even more demanding, but even the highest standard of airmanship in the prevailing conditions would be insufficient to save Knight.

Knight took off from Coningsby on 15 September 1943 at 23.58 hours in the wake of Holden and Martin, and all four Lancasters of the first wave remained in contact until reaching Nordhorn. Knight and his crew witnessed the end of Holden, and then Martin led them towards the town of Rheine after glimpsing the flare path of an airfield ahead through the mist. Flak at Rheine split the section up, and Martin believed initially that Knight had been shot down. Amazingly they came upon the correct target area and began searching for the aiming point. It was while flying a series of one-minute box circuits as they waited their turn to attack that Knight and his crew failed to spot treetops poking out of the fog. They ploughed through the branches, losing the use of both port engines as a result, and

The memorial stone on the roadside at Knight's crash site.

The trees that brought Les Knight down.

Les Knight's grave at Den Ham.

damaging control surfaces. Knight was left with no option but to seek permission to jettison the dead weight of the bomb and try to get home. By the time they approached the small Dutch town of Den Ham, it was becoming impossible to keep the Lancaster flying straight and level and Knight knew they would never negotiate the sea crossing. He dragged the Lancaster as high as he possibly could and his seven crew mates parachuted clear. Alone in the bomber, Knight tried to pull off a controlled forced landing in a field, but struck trees and nosed into the ground, where the wreckage burned furiously. Five of the crew managed to evade capture and get home within about six weeks.

## Tour Guide

Approaching from the direction of Osnabrück we travel along the A30 (E30) over the border into Holland, past Oldenzaal, heading towards Hengelo. We depart the A30 (E30) at the Hengelo exit and turn left onto the N36 towards Almelo. After Almelo we

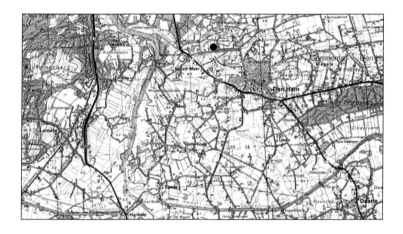

leave the N36 at the next major junction, turning left onto the N341 towards Den Ham/Ommen. As soon as we reach Den Ham we find the cemetery on the right where F/L Knight is buried. It is well worthwhile calling here to visit the grave and pay respects to a gallant pilot. We stay on the N341 out of Den Ham. At the first somewhat larger crossroads outside of the town, the Hammer Street leads off to the right. We follow this dead straight road until a boulder on the right-hand verge marks the crash site of F/L Knight's Lancaster. We are standing in front of a meadow, bounded by trees. To the right the treetops in the centre of the row of trees bear the imprint of a Lancaster's head-on profile. The impact robbed the stricken bomber of its flying speed, and it nosed into the meadow.

# CHAPTER 11

# S/L H.E. Maudslay
## ED937, AJ-Z
## Klein Netterden, North-east of Emmerich

## Dams Raid

Henry Maudslay was born in Royal Leamington Spa, Warwickshire, in July 1921. Four years later the family moved to the village of Sherbourne, a few miles south-west of Warwick. His parents were Reginald, who died in 1934, and Susan, and he had a sister, Margaret, who was eleven years' his senior. The Maudslay family was connected with both the Standard Motor Company and the Maudslay Motor Company. Henry was sent to preparatory school in Gloucestershire, and attended Eton College from 1935 to 1940. Here, he excelled as an athlete, both as a miler and as an oarsman, and his prowess was recognised in his election as Captain of Boats and Captain of Athletics during his final year. During this period, in 1937, the family moved to Foxhill Manor, an imposing house at Willersey in Worcestershire.

Having volunteered for the RAF, Maudslay was called up in July 1940, and after beginning elementary flying training

The author at Maudslay's crash site holding a piece of the wreckage.

in Yorkshire and Shropshire, he was posted to Canada under the Commonwealth Air Training Plan. He returned to the UK in February 1941, and after training on Hampdens at 25 OTU, he was posted to 44 Squadron at Waddington as a Pilot Officer in May. From then until early November he flew a total of twenty-nine operations, before being detached to Boscombe Down for Lancaster training. This period of his service is difficult to establish, but it seems that he was also detached to Rolls-Royce at Derby from 7 to 10 January 1942. He returned to 44 Squadron Conversion Flight in January as an instructor, and was promoted to Flying Officer on 29 January, the day before his DFC was gazetted. He seems to have been at Boscombe Down again from 9 to 15 February in some capacity connected with the Lancaster.

Maudslay did not carry out any further operational sorties until the first thousand-bomber raid on Cologne on the night of 30/31 May. For this momentous occasion he flew the Conversion Flight's Manchester L7430, an aircraft with a reputation as a 'hack'. Two nights later he took another 'hack', Manchester

L7480, to Essen for the second of the thousand-bomber raids, and completed the hat-trick by operating against Bremen in the third and final of these mammoth efforts on 25/26 June in Lancaster R5862.

In July he was posted to 1654 Conversion Unit at Wigsley, where 5 Group crews were converted to Lancasters, and here he came into contact with a number of future 617 Squadron recruits as they passed through his hands. He requested a return to operational duties at the earliest opportunity, and was posted to 50 Squadron at Skellingthorpe in January 1943.

He completed another thirteen operations from here as a Flight Lieutenant, before moving to Scampton and 617 Squadron as a Squadron Leader and B Flight commander. He took some of his crew with him, and picked up others along the way. John Marriott, the flight engineer, had previously flown with Drew Wyness at 50 Squadron and had notched up twenty-six operations. Wyness would also one day join 617 Squadron and lose his life as the result of a war crime in October 1944. Bill

Herr Johannes Doerwald in Emmerich, on the spot where his flak battery stood on the night that he, as a 16 year-old gun layer, was credited with bringing Maudslay down.

Maudslay's crash site near Emmerich.

Tytherleigh would fly to the Dams in Maudslay's front turret. Barely twenty-one years old, he was another graduate of 50 Squadron and already a veteran with over forty operations under his belt. Likewise, the navigator, Bob Urquhart, had completed almost a full tour with 50 Squadron. Mike Fuller, the bomb-aimer, had been at 106 Squadron until joining Maudslay at 50 Squadron, and he had a tally of twenty-seven operations in his logbook. The rear gunner was Norman Burrows, another man of experience from 50 Squadron. The wireless operator was Canadian Allan Cottam, who at thirty was the old man of the crew.

On 16 May 1943 Maudslay led the final section of the first wave away from Scampton at 21.59 hours, with Astell and Knight on either side. Following Astell's loss about fifteen minutes' flying time from the Möhne Lake, Maudslay and Knight arrived at the target in time to witness Hopgood's attack and subsequent destruction (see Chapter 9). They circled at the far end of the lake awaiting their turn to bomb if the dam was still intact after Young, Maltby and Shannon had made their attempts.

In the event they were not required, and flew on to the Eder, fifty miles to the east with Gibson, Young as his deputy and Shannon, who still had his Upkeep weapon on board. The bombing runs at the various targets had been planned from models and reconnaissance photographs, but the reality at the Eder was that there was insufficient time to attain the necessary height, speed and direction for an accurate attack. A paltry seven seconds was all that remained after they had turned hard to port over a spit of land jutting out into the lake, from which a line could be drawn to the centre of the dam. At least the dam was undefended, but the terrain made the approach and exit demanding in the extreme. The operational difficulties were amply demonstrated by Shannon's repeated inability to get into a position to deliver his Upkeep. The approach was via a cutting between hills to the right of Waldeck Castle perched high above the lake. It was then necessary to throttle back, apply flap and dive towards the spit on the opposite bank, before making the sharp turn to port to face the dam. Adjustments to speed, height and line took time in a heavy Lancaster, and there was just not enough distance remaining to achieve more than an approximation, and that was simply not good enough.

Maudslay's crash site with Emmerich to the right.

After a number of abortive attempts Gibson ordered Shannon to pull away and allow Maudslay to have a crack. Gibson was conscious that the operation was falling behind schedule, and that dawn might catch them still over enemy territory. In the light of what took place when Maudslay attacked the dam, a comment by Gibson in his book *Enemy Coast Ahead* might be significant. He speaks of Maudslay flying towards the castle and the cutting, but pulling away suddenly before resuming his approach. One wonders if perhaps the belly of the Lancaster, and indeed, the bomb, had brushed against treetops or some other ground obstacle. At 01.45 hours onlookers watched Maudslay race across the water and saw the bomb fall away at the last moment, striking the parapet of the dam and exploding in a blinding flash on impact. AJ-Z was silhouetted just above and beyond the blast, and the immediate impression was that Maudslay had blown himself up. Amazingly, he was able to respond fairly positively to the second of two enquiries by Gibson about his state of health, and all that remained for him to do was turn for home.

At 01.57 hours Group received a coded message by R/T from Maudslay notifying the outcome of his attack. It seems certain that AJ-Z had sustained damage, but how much and its nature will never be known. At around 02.30 hours AJ-Z approached the town of Emmerich, nestling on the east bank of the Rhine. Ahead and to the north the Dutch border lay within touching distance and Maudslay had to decide whether to cross the town or skirt it on its northern side. Emmerich contained sensitive oil storage facilities and was defended by a ring of light flak batteries. We have broadly similar reports from two men at different flak batteries that tell us that the Lancaster attempted to fly directly over the town, but was beaten back by the ground fire and set ablaze, eventually crashing in a field north of the town.

## Tour Guide

I made my first visit to the site at Klein Netterden in May 2001. Three months previously Andreas and Horst had located the site, and with the aid of Horst's metal detector, which became known as his 'machine', some pieces of wreckage were recovered from the snow-covered ground. Andreas and I returned to Emmerich in 2003, this time meeting up with *Herr* Johannes Doerwald, who,

2004 tour at Maudslay's crash site.

as a sixteen year-old gun layer, was decorated for bringing down
Maudslay's Lancaster. We visited the site of his flak battery and
listened to his account of the events of that memorable night sixty
years earlier. It has to be said, that it differed markedly from those
written at the time of the incident.

We travel on the A3 (E35) towards the Dutch frontier as far as
Junction 3 (Emmerich). At the junction with the B220 we turn left
heading towards the town of Emmerich. We follow this road,
carrying straight on at the first crossroads until, passing through
a small wood, we reach a second crossroads, which is an intersection with the K16. We turn left onto the K16 and head towards
Klein Netterden still surrounded by the wooded area. We travel
along the rural K16 and take the fourth road on our left. Now we
follow this narrow tarmac road until we encounter a small crossroads. Here we turn left, and soon thereafter meet a fork in the
road. Keep left at this fork. On either side now are large meadows,
and it is time to park the car in one of the gateways on the verge.
We are seeking the last meadow on the right-hand side of
the road, and must walk along until finding a rampart across the

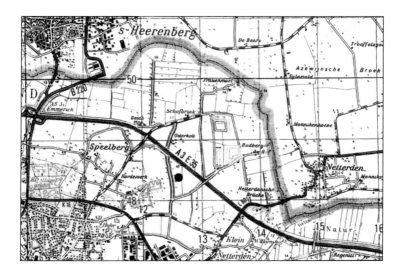

narrow ditch. In the background bordering the field to the left is the A3 motorway, just beyond which lies Holland. S/L Maudslay's Lancaster crashed in the middle of this field. During the construction of an irrigation channel and a well after the war, pieces of the wreckage were found, but nothing now remains to be unearthed.

# CHAPTER 12

# P/O W.H.T. Ottley
## ED910, AJ-C
## Hövel-Bockum. North-west of Hamm

### Dams Raid

P/O Warner Ottley was born in Battersea, London, in 1923, and was educated at Hurstpierpoint College on the south coast. At the time of his service with Bomber Command he was resident in Letchworth in Hertfordshire, although his parents lived at Herne Bay in Kent. Coincidentally, his rear gunner, Sgt Fred Tees, also lived in Letchworth. Despite being one of the youngest pilots to join 617 Squadron, he had completed a full tour of operations with 207 Squadron. The citation for his DFC, which was gazetted posthumously in June 1945, confirms that he was a press-on type. It refers to an attack on Wilhelmshaven, when he made three runs across the target to ensure accuracy, and a gardening (mining) sortie, during which his aircraft was damaged by flak ships. Ottley is said to have applied for a posting to the Pathfinder Force on completion of his tour with 207 Squadron, but no vacancy existing, he then approached Gibson personally. It is inconceivable, however, that no room could be found in the Pathfinder Force for such an experienced pilot. Shannon had just been posted to 83 Squadron at Wyton for

PFF (Pathfinder Force) training, and W/C 'Hamish' Mahaddie, known as the Pathfinder Horse Thief, was employed specifically by Pathfinder chief Bennett to recruit crews on an on-going basis to compensate for the almost nightly attrition. Ottley's reputation as a 'press-on type' would have had Mahaddie beating a path to his door, so we are forced to conclude that his application to join 8 Group was either a myth, or, perhaps, it coincided with a personal approach to Gibson, who got in with the first offer.

Ottley was a member of the third and final wave of Operation *Chastise*, and remained at Scampton until his take-off in the lead of the section at 00.09 hours. He made landfall safely at the enemy coast having followed the southerly route first ploughed by wave one, then picked his way gingerly across Holland and into Germany. At 02.28 hours Group sent a coded message to Ottley directing him towards his last resort target, the Lister Dam. Ottley acknowledged at 02.31 hours, then received another signal changing his destination to the Sorpe. By this time he was at a position north-west of the town of Hamm, an important railway junction with extensive marshalling yards. The local

Ottley and some of his crew. Ottley is 2nd from the right.

The original memorial at Ottley's crash site.

defenders had already been stirred into action that night by McCarthy's stumbling back and forth across the town seeking a route home. He somehow survived, but Ottley and his crew were less fortunate. Ottley turned south towards the Sorpe reservoir too early, and headed into the teeth of the town's forward light flak batteries in fields. At 02.35 hours the Lancaster was hit in a fuel tank, causing a fierce fire. The bomber turned away from Hamm, flying west to east across the villages of Hövel and Bockum, before an explosion tore off the wing. The bomb exploded on impact on the edge of a wood, flinging the rear turret and its occupant clear. Miraculously, Fred Tees survived, burned and shocked, and was soon taken prisoner without resistance. The local people are convinced that Ottley remained at the controls to avoid causing casualties in the villages, and they viewed him as a hero. An appealing thought though this is, Ottley would have been thinking first of the survival of his crew, and seeking a field to put the Lancaster down in as controlled a way as possible.

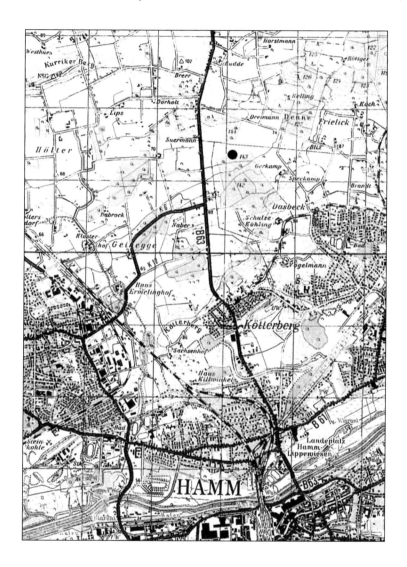

## Tour Guide

We travel along the A2 (E34) from the direction of Oberhausen heading towards Hannover as far as Junction 18 (Hamm). From the slip road we turn left onto the B63 and head towards

Hamm/Münster. We drive through Hamm, passing over the River Lippe and carry on towards Münster. After passing through the village of Kötterberg we encounter a wooded area on our right. We pass over a bridge spanning a stream with the wood still on our right. As we reach the end of the wood and see a road on our left, we park our car on the right-hand verge. We now look for a track on the right side of the road, running at right angles to the B63 leading to the wood across a field. It is possible to take a car along this track, but it is not recommended if the ground is sodden. The track enters the wood, and we pick up a number of possible paths. Keep to the left as the crash site of P/O Ottley's Lancaster lies on the very edge of the wood. It consists of a crater, above which stands a new wooden cross and the memorial stone mentioned in Chapter 1. The original cross had become rotten after many years in the frequently water-logged crater.

# CHAPTER 13

# F/L H.S. Wilson
## JA898, KC-X
## Near Ladbergen by the Dortmund-Ems Canal

### Dortmund-Ems Canal Raid

Harold Wilson was among the first to be posted to 617 Squadron, having served thus far with 44 (Rhodesia) Squadron. He was another man in his late twenties, and, therefore, was a little older than the average aircrew member arriving at the new squadron. He was a Pilot Officer when he began his first tour at Waddington after leaving 1654 Conversion Unit with all but one of his future 617 Squadron crew three days before Christmas 1942. Air gunner Sgt Payne was posted in from 1660 Conversion Unit to join them on 1 January 1943. Wilson's first operation was as second pilot to a F/O Walker on 8 January 1943, when Duisburg was the target for 1 and 5 Group Lancasters as part of the Oboe trials programme. He flew as crew captain for the first time against Cologne on the night of 2/3 February, and forty-eight hours' later carried a bomb bay full of 4-lb incendiaries to Turin. A trip to Lorient was followed by a raid on Wilhelmshaven on 11/12 February, during which two enemy night fighters were evaded through the excellent work of both gunners. Other operations in February took Wilson and his crew to Bremen, Nuremberg, Cologne and St Nazaire, although Sgt Payne was substituted for the last three of these, possibly through illness. The destination for the crew on 1/2 March was Berlin, and then came the opening salvo of the Ruhr campaign at Essen on the night of 5/6 March, to be followed by Munich on the 9/10th and the second Essen raid on the 12/13th. This, Wilson's final operation with 44 Squadron, almost ended in a collision with a Ju 88, but good co-operation between pilot and mid-upper gunner saved the day. This brought Wilson's operations tally to thirteen, by which time he was a Flying Officer. He and his crew arrived at Scampton on 24 March, and he was probably by then an acting Flight Lieutenant.

Wilson's crew trained for Operation *Chastise*, but did not take part, we are told, because of illness in the crew. In any event, only nineteen serviceable Lancasters existed for the twenty-one crews, so two would have missed out anyway. Wilson's first operation with the squadron was the shuttle raid on an electrical transformer station at Aquata Scrivia on 15/16 July, one of two similar targets for the night. On the way home on the night of 24/25 July, having spent the intervening period at Blida in North Africa, he bombed the docks at Leghorn. Wilson was the last of Holden's section to depart Coningsby for the Dortmund-Ems Canal, his take-off timed at 23.59 hours. Having reached the target area he seemed to find his bearings very quickly, and was heard to ask Allsebrook, the new leader after Holden's loss at Nordhorn, for permission to make his attack. This was granted, but his bomb was still on board when he crashed close to the canal's eastern bank at around 02.12 hours.

The flak defences around the canal had been strengthened earlier in the war because of the importance of this waterway to Germany's communications system. On this night, however, the flak batteries were ordered to remain dormant because of *Luftwaffe* operations over England out of the nearby base at Handorf. However, after repeated incursions across his beat the flak commander could contain himself no longer and gave the order to open fire when a Lancaster loomed out of the fog close enough for him to read the code letters on its fuselage. Wilson was a sitting duck, and the Lancaster caught fire immediately.

The trees hit by Wilson's Lancaster at Kötterheinricks.

Wilson's crash site on the morning after. The trees in the background have been stripped of their leaves by the blast from the bomb. Both photographs were taken by Herr Wibbeler, who was a 21 year-old soldier at home on leave when these events took place, and they are reproduced with his kind permission.

This was witnessed by the rear gunner in Knight's aircraft as they were about to begin another box circuit. Wilson staggered on, clipping a line of trees, before scraping over the roof of the Wibbeler homestead a few hundred yards further on. Finally, he came down in a field bordered by trees with the canal on his starboard side, and the wreckage burned furiously. Some fifteen minutes later the bomb exploded, scattering the wreckage around.

## Tour Guide

Andreas, Horst and I went to the site during my visit in May 2002. By chance, *Herr* Wibbeler was about to mow his lawn as we drove by his house, and we stopped to enquire about the precise location of the crash site. He said he would come with us to show us the field in question, where he also introduced us to the farmer who owned it. Again we encountered friendliness and co-operation, although the farmer jokingly said he would

The Dortmund-Ems Canal near Ladbergen close to the spot chosen for the 617 Squadron attack.

The Dortmund-Ems Canal looking north towards Ladbergen.

claim 90 per cent of anything we found. As soon as Horst's 'machine' was activated we began to find pieces of wreckage. Just below the surface we uncovered small items of aluminium, Perspex and complete .303 shells, some of them welded together by the intense heat of the fire following the crash. Incredibly, though, we found something else, which had also been in the ground for almost fifty-nine years, and had survived the plough literally dozens of times. It was a 9 carat gold signet ring, which we assumed had belonged to one of the crew, and *Herr* Wibbeler agreed that it was unlikely to have come from a German source. When I got home to Lutterworth I took it to a local jeweller, who confirmed that it had been manufactured by LW & Sons, and had been hallmarked in London in 1939. At that time it would have carried a retail price of about £1, roughly 20 per cent of an average weekly income. It was hoped that the ring could be reunited with the family to whom it rightfully belongs, and Dambuster historian Alex Bateman accordingly approached relatives of six of the crew by letter, inviting them to come forward. Sadly, they all declined the opportunity to take the matter further.

The River Glane underpass at the Dortmund-Ems canal.

The River Glane underpass at the Dortmund-Ems canal.

Herr Wibbeler, who with his father was the first to reach the scene of Wilson's crash.

The Petwood Hotel at Woodhall Spa in Lincolnshire is a shrine to 617 Squadron, and receives many visitors with an interest in the subject. It also hosts 617 Squadron reunions, and is the natural home for artefacts relating to the squadron's exploits. For this reason I offered the ring and small pieces of wreckage from five of the Lancasters lost on the Dams Raid on indefinite loan and they are now on display in the officers' bar.

Coming from the direction of Münster we travel along the A1 (E37) in the direction of Osnabrück. We leave the A1 (E37) at Junction 74 (Ladbergen). The slip road ends at the B475, onto which we turn left heading towards Saerbeck/*Flughafen* Münster/Osnabrück. Shortly before the B475 crosses the Dortmund-Ems Canal, a narrow slip road on the left takes us on a tight right-hand bend to meet a T-junction, which is the K11 proper. We turn left onto the K11, and follow it as it passes over a small bridge over the River Aa tributary. Shortly afterwards we meet a crossroads with a sign pointing to the Schumacher-museum, and ahead we can see a bridge taking the road back

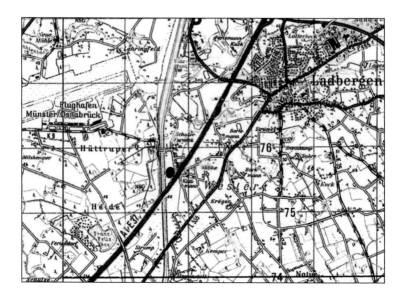

across the canal. At this crossroads we turn right onto a narrow road and drive towards the Schumachermuseum. We remain on this road as it winds towards and then runs parallel with the canal embankment. We pass the museum, which is the home of *Herr* Wibbeler, an eyewitness to the Lancaster's crash, and continue until reaching some houses, one of which belongs to a farmer who owns the crash site field. On our right is the very field into which F/L Wilson's JA898 crashed. On the way back, it is worth taking the opportunity to scale the embankment and stand on the canal towpath. To the right is the underpass carrying the River Glane under the canal, and this was the target for 5 Group attacks in late 1944 and early 1945. There is a bronze plaque on the underpass commemorating the fifty local victims of these raids.

# CHAPTER 14

# S/L H.M. Young
## ED887, AJ-A
## In the Sea off Castricum-aan-Zee

### Dams Raid

Henry Melvin Young was born on 20 May 1915 in Belgravia, London. His father was a qualified solicitor working within the family legal business, but had joined the army during the Great War, and at the time of Henry's birth was a 2nd Lieutenant in the 4th Battalion, The Queen's Royal West Surrey Regiment. His mother, Fanny, hailed from Los Angeles, where her family was part of the social set, and she met her future husband while he and a friend were travelling the world before settling down to their careers. Both Fanny and Henry senior were talented athletes, she at tennis and he at rowing, particularly during his time at Oxford. Henry decided to remain in America to practise law, and he married Fanny in 1913. They soon moved to England, however, in time for the arrival of Henry junior and his sister, Angela, but the austerity of post-war England was not to Fanny's liking, and the family returned to California. Some time later Henry senior returned alone to England, leaving Fanny and the children in Palmdale, California, where Henry junior was raised. He was educated at Kent College, Connecticut, where he

A less familiar view of the breached Möhne Dam taken from
the wet side after the torrent had subsided.

met his future wife, Priscilla Rawson. In time, he joined his father in England and attended Westminster school, before following in Henry senior's footsteps by going up to Oxford, and while there, joining the Oxford University Rowing Club. This led to his selection at number seven in the crew for the 1938 University Boat Race, in which Oxford defeated Cambridge by two lengths.

Young joined the RAF Volunteer Reserve in August 1939 as a Pilot Officer, and after training was posted on 10 June 1940 to 4 Group's 102 Squadron to fly Whitleys. By now a Flying Officer, here he was a colleague of P/O Leonard Cheshire, another young man who was to make a name for himself both before and after joining 617 Squadron. Young's first thirteen operations were flown as second pilot to a P/O Painter, and it was not until September, when 102 Squadron was loaned to Coastal Command for patrol duties, that he flew as crew captain for the first time. During a patrol on 7 October, while on detachment to Aldergrove in Northern Ireland, engine failure forced Young to ditch his Whitley in the Atlantic. He and his crew bobbed up and down in the swell for some twenty-two hours, before rescue came at the hands of the Royal Navy's HMS *St Mary*.

The squadron returned to Bomber Command after a six-week tour of duty with webbed feet, and on the night of 23/24 November, Young found himself operating against Turin. On the way home he ran out of fuel after more than eleven hours' aloft, and was forced to ditch once more, this time off the south coast of Devon. He and his crew paddled ashore in their dinghy, and as a result of this, and his previous conspicuous devotion to dinghy drill for his crew, which had twice proved well founded, 'Dinghy' became the name by which he was universally known, and the name he would carry to his untimely death.

At the completion of his tour early in 1941, Young was posted to 10 OTU as an instructor, and from there to 22 OTU. His DFC was gazetted on 9 May, and he was promoted to Flight Lieutenant in August. In September he joined 104 Squadron, a 4 Group unit at Driffield operating the Merlin-powered Wellington Mk II, and commanded by W/C Beare, whom Young knew as a flight commander from his 102 Squadron days.

During October a number of squadrons sent a detachment to the Middle East to join 238 Wing of 205 Group, leaving a small

Dinghy Young's Lancaster lies on a sandbank off the Dutch
coast at Castricum-aan-Zee, having been brought down by flak
when on the very brink of safety.

home echelon to rebuild. Young was among the fifteen crew-strong 104 Squadron element departing for Malta on 18 October, for what was intended to be a two-month tour of duty. In the event, the move for the squadron proved to be permanent, and after something of a dispute, the overseas element retained the 104 number, while the home echelon was renumbered 158 Squadron, which, as a Halifax unit, would go on to become a mainstay of 4 Group for the remainder of the war. The detachment arrived at Luqa on 20 October, and Young and his crew were operating against Naples on the following night. In January 1942, the squadron moved to Kabrit in Egypt, and then on to landing grounds closer to its targets.

On 1 June Young was promoted to Squadron Leader, and he and his crew were rested from operations. He was not immediately posted home, but took up duties at HQ 205 Group for a short period. In August he went to America, where he married Priscilla on the 10th. A Bar to his DFC was gazetted on 18 September recognising fifty-one sorties, and then on 15 October he was sent to America for special duties.

On Young's return to England he rejoined Bomber Command, and was posted to 57 Squadron at Scampton on 13 March 1943, the day after the second operation of the recently begun Ruhr campaign. The next round of major operations was not destined to begin until the final week of the month, and this would have allowed Young time to settle in at his new unit, had his posting to 617 Squadron not intervened. Young's reputation as a no-nonsense, efficient organiser was known to Gibson, as was his ability to sink a pint of beer faster than anyone else on earth!

Much of the responsibility for the training for Operation *Chastise* fell on Young's shoulders. On 16 May 1943 he led the second section of the first wave away from Scampton at 21.47 hours with Maltby and Shannon, and they arrived safely at the Möhne Lake just as Gibson was making his attack. Frustration was beginning to mount by the time Young was called in to make his bombing run. Gibson's bomb had fallen short, Hopgood's had skipped over the dam and destroyed the power-house, but had not scratched the wall itself, and Martin's had veered off to the left and exploded ineffectively on the muddy shore.

In contrast, Young's run at 00.43 hours was perfect, and the bomb struck the centre of the dam wall before sinking in precisely the manner demanded by Wallis, the weapon's inventor. It was not immediately clear what toll the explosion hard against the masonry had exacted, and when the water had calmed sufficiently the wall appeared to be intact. In fact, just as Wallis had predicted, the dam had been fatally weakened, and this became evident to Maltby as he closed in on the target to deliver his Upkeep bomb. The crest of the dam was actually beginning to crumble as his bomb fell away in what was another near-perfect delivery. The weight of water would have rolled the wall over anyway, but Maltby's bomb sealed its fate.

Young then accompanied Gibson and the others with a bomb still on board to the Eder reservoir, where he remained in attendance until that target, too, succumbed to the genius of Wallis and the skill and professionalism of the airmen of Bomber Command.

Little is known of Young's return journey across Germany and Holland to the safety of the North Sea, only that the heroic homecoming so richly deserved was not to be. Like Holden after him, and the vast majority of main-force pilots, Young was not accustomed to low flying, and it is understood that he was not comfortable with the practice. The other returnees scraped their bellies on the dunes as they swept over the coast and raced for home a few feet off the waves. Young approached the sandy shoreline at Castricum-aan-Zee way too high, and was brought down by the last few squirts of flak available to ensnare him. The Lancaster crashed on a sand bar a hundred yards or so off the beach at 02.59 hours, the last of the eight missing bombers, declared in a BBC news bulletin later that morning as the cost of a highly successful raid on two German dams.

## Tour Guide

When Andreas and I arrived at Castricum-aan-Zee in May 2003 it was cold and blustery, and low cloud hampered visibility over the sea. The beach stretches for miles to the north and south of Castricum, and numbered stout wooden marker posts, or *paals*, stand at one-kilometre intervals with others in between counting off each 250 metres. It is only possible to access the beach at certain defined points, because the high sand dunes separating the sea from the countryside formed part of the Atlantic Wall during the war and were heavily mined. No one knows for certain whether any remain. A Dutch researcher, Paul Patist, had told Andreas that Young came down at *paal* 47, a little to the south of the beach access point, where we took advantage of the cafés to fortify ourselves before venturing into the strong wind. A lady at a nearby table confirmed the position of the Lancaster's crash. She said that the wreckage had remained there until 1953, when the violent storm that devastated our south-east coast and Canvey Island carried it away and distributed it all along the beach. The tide was just beginning to ebb as we walked to the spot, so most of the beach was under water. We could tell from the breakers a hundred yards out that a sandbank existed, and this was where the aircraft came to rest.

S/L Dinghy Young and his crew are buried in the small military section of the General cemetery at Bergen (not to be confused with Bergen-op-Zoom) in Holland, and it is well worth a visit. Six of the graves lie in line, but one is separated from the others. To find the crash site we drive south on the main route

Paal 47 looking out towards the sand bar upon which Young's Lancaster crashed.

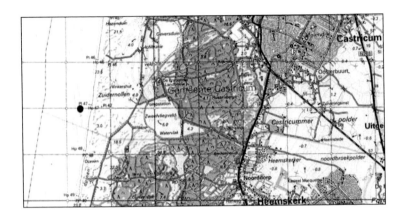

out of Bergen until reaching a crossroads. Turn right onto the
Zeeweg, which is signposted for Castricum-aan-Zee. As we
approach we see buildings ahead atop the dunes and a car park
off to the left. From the car park it is a short walk to the beach. A
café on either side of the entrance to the beach will provide
sustenance, during the season, for the walk to the crash site.
Turn left and begin to walk in a southerly direction, taking note
of the wooden posts set at 250-metre distances. Each kilometre
post or *paal* bears a number, and we are looking for *paal* 47. This
is a considerable and bracing walk of about two kilometres
along what is often a windswept beach, and might involve a
round trip of an hour or more. It is not recommended for those
with a medical condition.

# Afterword

I cannot, of course, complete this guide without providing the means to find the crash site and grave of W/C Guy Gibson, and indeed the Commonwealth War Graves Cemeteries containing the remains of the majority of those who lost their lives on the two operations detailed in the foregoing chapters. Gibson and his navigator, S/L Jim Warwick, lie side by side in the Catholic cemetery at Steenbergen in Holland, the place where their Mosquito came down in unresolved circumstances on the night of 19/20 September 1944, following a raid on the twin towns of Mönchengladbach and Rheydt, for which Gibson had acted as Master Bomber. Steenbergen is situated 24 kilometres from the Belgian frontier. From the St Gumanuskerk in the centre of the town travel to the far end of the *Markt*, before turning left into Grote Kerkstraat. After 150 metres this leads into the *Kerkplein*. Follow the road through the *Kerkplein*, leaving it at the other side into Kruispoort. Continue approximately half a kilometre to find the cemetery on the right-hand side. The two headstones are positioned on the left side of the first avenue from the entrance. The actual crash site is located in an industrial estate on Gibsonstraat within the yard of a timber merchant, and is marked by a wooden post on the pavement opposite.

Remaining in Holland we travel towards the town of Bergen-op-Zoom to visit the graves of F/O Burpee and his crew. There are two war cemeteries almost next to each other, one of them

Gibson and
Warwick, who lie
side-by-side in the
Catholic cemetery
at Steenbergen in
southern Holland.

for Canadians. Burpee and his crew, however, are in the other one. The cemeteries lie 3 kilometres to the east of the town centre on Ruytershoveweg, which runs parallel with the A58 Bergen-op-Zoom to Roosendaal motorway. Travelling along the A58 we take the Bergen-op-Zoom exit, which leads onto Rooseveltlaan. At the first crossroads the cemeteries are signposted to the right. There is a further signposted right turn after 1 kilometre, and the cemeteries are located 2 kilometres along this road on the left-hand side.

Rheinberg Cemetery contains the remains of Hopgood and four of his crew. It also contains the crew of Cyril Anderson, who returned to 49 Squadron after Operation *Chastise* but failed to return from a raid on Mannheim on the night of 23/24 September 1943. The town of Rheinberg is 24 kilometres north of Krefeld and 13 kilometres south of Wesel. The cemetery can be found 3 kilometres south of the town centre on the road to Kamp

George Holden's headstone at Reichswald Commonwealth War Graves Cemetery.

Sir Arthur Harris, C-in-C Bomber Command from February 1942 until war's end. Experience made him sceptical about the likely success of Operation Chastise, but his opposition was overruled. He was also against the use of heavy bombers in low-level operations. The Dams and Dortmund-Ems Canal losses confirmed his fears.

Lintfort. Leaving the A57 motorway at the Rheinberg exit, take the B510 (Rheinberger Strasse) towards Kamp Lintfort. The cemetery is a short distance further along on the right-hand side. The remaining final resting places, with one exception, can be found in the cemetery at Reichswald. It is situated 5 kilometres south-west of Kleve. The L484 runs south-west from Kleve directly through the Reichswald forest, and passes the cemetery on the left, with parking available directly opposite the main gate. Alternatively, if approaching along the B504, turn onto the L484 at a signposted crossroads right on the edge of the forest.

The entire process of researching and writing *Dambusters* was exhilarating, and Andreas and I were able to uncover much new information, some of it bringing to light for the first time the final moments of the lives of some very gallant young men from Britain and the Commonwealth. Their like will not be seen

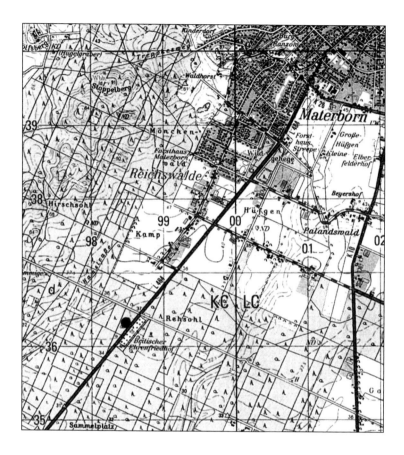

again, because the world that created them and which they graced, like them, has passed into history. New generations of their families live on, and I'm sure, take pride in the fact that their forebears were part of the most famous squadron in RAF history. All those of us involved in the writing of this book and in the uncovering of the history contained herein humbly share that pride.